CASE STUDIES IN
CULTURAL ANTHROPOLOGY

GENERAL EDITORS
George and Louise Spindler
STANFORD UNIVERSITY

K'UN SHEN
A Taiwan Village

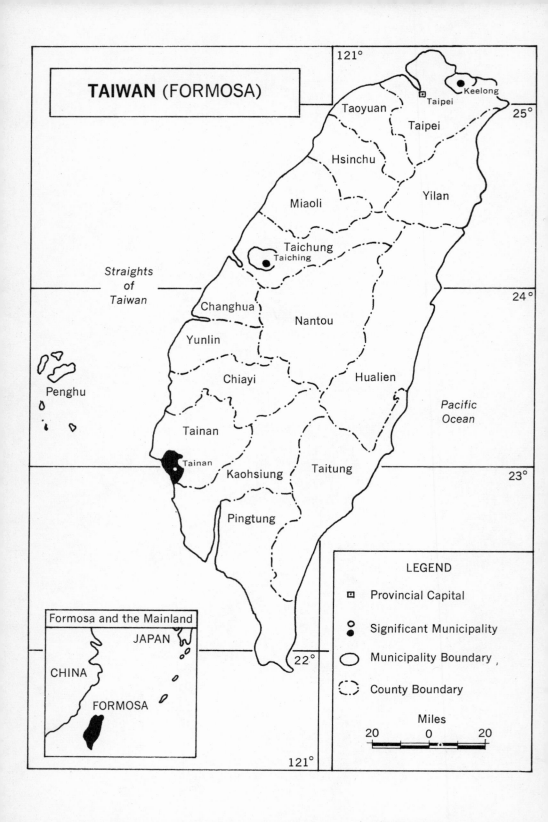

TAIWAN (FORMOSA)

121°

Taoyuan

Taipei

25°

Taipei

Keelong

Hsinchu

Yilan

Miaoli

Taichung
Taiching

Straights
of
Taiwan

24°

Changhua

Nantou

Yunlin

Chiayi

Hualien

Pacific
Ocean

Penghu

Tainan

Tainan

23°

Kaohsiung

Taitung

Pingtung

LEGEND

Provincial Capital

Significant Municipality

Municipality Boundary

County Boundary

Formosa and the Mainland

JAPAN

CHINA

FORMOSA

22°

Miles

20   0   20

121°

K'UN SHEN
A Taiwan Village

By

NORMA DIAMOND

University of Michigan

HOLT, RINEHART AND WINSTON

NEW YORK   CHICAGO   SAN FRANCISCO   ATLANTA
DALLAS   MONTREAL   TORONTO   LONDON   SYDNEY

Copyright © 1969 by Holt, Rinehart and Winston, Inc.
All rights reserved
Library of Congress Catalog Card Number: 69–17650
SBN: 03–080960–6
Printed in the United States of America
1 2 3 4 5 6 7 8 9

Foreword

About the Series

These case studies in cultural anthropology are designed to bring to students, in beginning and intermediate courses in the social sciences, insights into the richness and complexity of human life as it is lived in different ways and in different places. They are written by men and women who have lived in the societies they write about, and who are professionally trained as observers and interpreters of human behavior. The authors are also teachers, and in writing their books they have kept the students who will read them foremost in their minds. It is our belief that when an understanding of ways of life very different from one's own is gained, abstractions and generalizations about social structure, cultural values, subsistence techniques, and the other universal categories of human social behavior become meaningful.

About the Author

Norma Diamond is an assistant professor in the Department of Anthropology at the University of Michigan. She studied anthropology at the University of Wisconsin and at Cornell, and received her doctorate from Cornell. She has spent two and a half years in Taiwan, first doing language study under an Inter-University Fellowship for Field Training in Chinese and then a year and a half of field research under a grant from the Ford Foundation. She has also been the recipient of a Fels Fellowship. Currently, she is engaged in research on nineteenth- and early twentieth-century mainland China.

About the Book

This is the first study in this series of a Chinese community. K'un Shen is a fishing village on the island of Taiwan, the province which has served as a retreat for Chiang Kai-shek and the Kuomintang since 1948. However, the people of K'un Shen were there long before this recent influx from the mainland occurred. They are the descendants of seventeenth- and eighteenth-century migrants from southeastern China. Though their culture has not remained static since that time and has undergone modifications in adaptation to the ecology and sociopolitical situation in Taiwan, their way of life represents one of the significant variants of traditional Chinese peasant culture.

The people of K'un Shen do not have strong national identifications. The segments of the mainland population migrating to Taiwan after the Communists gained control were largely businessmen from Westernized urban centers and were foreign in language, behavior, and values to the folk culture of villages like K'un Shen. They are not a source of identification for the peasants. The villagers see themselves primarily as citizens of K'un Shen and of the surrounding region. They do see themselves as having some relation to China's cultural heritage, but they do not, as Dr. Diamond states, "see themselves as being fully in and of present-day Chinese society, either in its mainland version or in its urban version in Taiwan."

The author provides us with a very direct and clear picture of the way of life in K'un Shen. Western readers unfamiliar with Chinese peasant life may be startled to find strong parallels to the puritanical beliefs and practices of an earlier American culture. Mothers never discuss any topic related to sex with their children, including child bearing. Girls are taught extreme modesty in dress and demeanor from the earliest years. There is very little dating, even today, among young people. Moderation and control furnish the keynotes of the culture. The expression of emotionality of any sort is discouraged—pleasure, love, hatred, or rage; and further, great value is placed upon hard work and saving time. Less time is spent on recreation and celebration than in many other Chinese peasant communities. Religious observances centering upon the Lung-shan temple in the center of the village provide most of the enlivenment. Dr. Diamond's description of these affairs provides sharp contrasts to the otherwise moderate and repressed tone of village life.

This case study is also notable for the detailed account of the treatment a person receives from childhood to adulthood. This subculture is adult oriented. Children are not expected to speak up or offer any ideas or suggestions to adults. They are never praised, even when they succeed, for parents feel that praise would cause complacency. The dynamics of the parent/child relationship produce children lacking in self-confidence.

The economic basis of life in K'un Shen is, largely, sea fishing, done close to shore and on well-made bamboo rafts powered by oars and sail. The author provides very specific information on the techniques and equipment used, the difficulties encountered, and the rewards gained. Many households also own and cultivate fish ponds from which a substantial income is derived. The varieties of fish raised, and the conditions and rewards of their cultivation, are described.

Of particular interest today, where most primitive and folk societies are undergoing radical transformation, is the relatively unchanging character of K'un Shen culture. Since the inhabitants have a strong respect for "science"—for learning and using new techniques when old ones fail and attributing failure more often to natural consequences than to "fate"—the reader is led to ask why more extensive change has not occurred. There seem to be many factors militating against change in K'un Shen. Technological change is held in check by the fact that some techniques, such as pond cultivation, have reached the upper limit of improvement for productivity. Other major changes, such as the adoption of mechanized equipment for deep-sea fishing, are held in check by the lack of personal and communal funds for the purchase of expensive equipment. Other factors may include the villager's attitude toward education, which is regarded as a luxury appropriate to only a "special" few. Children in school are given little encouragement or help, and are not praised when they succeed. Of particular importance as an inhibitor of change is the strong role of the family, whose influential members are mainly traditional and illiterate. The family is responsible for managing all important events in one's life from birth through death; and the family is an important link with the supernatural, as all religious ceremonials, offerings, and support of shrines are "family affairs." Perhaps certain characteristics of the present Mainland government and its policies may be understood as a massive attempt to destroy similar attitudes and institutions that act as strongly conservative forces, and that can be seen in microcosm in the village of K'un Shen.

GEORGE AND LOUISE SPINDLER
General Editors

Stanford, Calif.
January 1969

Contents

K'UN SHEN
A Taiwan Village

1

The Village and Its Background

The Setting

THE GREAT LAND MASS that is China has shown an amazing uniformity of tradition over thousands of years in time and over thousands of miles in space. This continuity and unity are found most markedly in the philosophy, political theory, and ethics that are subsumed under the tradition of Confucian thought and in the Buddhist and Taoist impacts on art, poetry, and religion. The Great Traditions of Imperial China were fostered and carried on by its elite or "gentry class." The gentry were drawn primarily from the great landowner families, those who could afford to educate their sons in the Confucian classics, dynastic histories, and literature of the past. After lengthy study, the sons could take a series of government-regulated examinations which won them political office and privilege within the society, both for themselves and for their families. These elite families formed a small but forceful ruling group, wielding both economic and political powers.

Traditional China, and by that we mean China from 221 B.C. to A.D. 1911, was basically a two-class society. Some 85 percent or more of the population were peasants, involved in agriculture and related occupations such as handicrafts and fishing. They ranged from impoverished tenant farmers to comfortable landlords with aspiration of gaining gentry status. For the most part illiterate, they had less of a share in the ideology of the Great Traditions. Even so, Confucian ideals of family organization and state authority were transmitted to them through membership in lineage organizations that included both peasant and gentry households, or through contact with gentry members living in the villages. At the same time, geographical factors, dialect diversity, difficulties in transportation, and the like made for a proliferation of peasant subcultures, each with some variations in custom and belief that diverged from the over-all pattern of peasant China.

This study is concerned with one local variation, and therefore should not be taken as typical of China as a whole. Moreover, since it is a study of a present-day

1

community, one which has been subjected to modernizing influences for some 60 years, it should not be mistaken for a picture of traditional China. Rather, it should be seen as an example of one type of Chinese community, in a state of change.

This study is concerned with a village we shall call K'un Shen, which is located in Taiwan, a large island some 120 miles east of the China coast. Taiwan represents one of the last frontiers of the Chinese empire. Except for a small surviving group of aborigines of Malayo-Polynesian stock (similar to groups in the northern Philippines), the population derives from seventeenth- and eighteenth-century migrants from the coastal province of Fukien in southeastern China. The first Chinese governor of the province and the first major waves of colonists arrived in the mid-sixteenth century. Over the years, control of the province shifted. The Dutch held the province from 1624 to 1662. It was then seized by the troops of Koxinga, Ming loyalists resisting the Ch'ing dynasty (1644–1911). This rebel government maintained itself until 1683, when Imperial control by the Ch'ing was reestablished. In 1895 China lost Taiwan to the Japanese, and it remained a Japanese colony until the end of World War II. Taiwan was returned to China, then under the rule of the Nationalist government (Kuomintang). It became a place of retreat for Chiang Kai-shek and the Kuomintang in 1948–1949, when the Chinese Communists gained control of the Mainland. Taiwan today is both politically and culturally Chinese, but it bears some marks of the long period of Japanese colonial rule.

The area of southwestern Taiwan where our village of K'un Shen is located was the earliest to be settled. Under the Dutch, under Koxinga, and under the Ch'ing dynasty it was the area of the capital and the area most effectively under government control. Tainan, the former capital, has been stripped of political power since the turn of the century. However, it has continued to grow, to a present-day population of over 300,000. This figure includes a number of farming and fishing villages within a few hours' walk of the city proper, including the village of K'un Shen. The city is an important marketing center for agricultural and fisheries produce. It also holds a number of light industries such as paper, modern textiles, clothing, sugar refining, and food processing, as well as continuing some of the older traditional handicrafts such as embroidery and wood-carving. Moreover, the city is a religious and educational center. Its temples and monasteries are well maintained, and it can boast a number of middle schools (high schools), colleges, libraries, and museums.

The area is one of rich agricultural plains, a farming region which produces rice, cane, sweet potatoes, and a variety of vegetables and fruits. Along the coast the soils are too sandy and saline to permit the growing of crops, except for the sweet potato, and the land is converted into fish ponds. The climate is subtropical. During the winter months the temperature falls between 54°F and 77°F. Between April and November it is usually over 72°F with a summer average of 82°F. The relative summer coolness is aided by sea breezes, the summer typhoons, and summer rains.

K'un Shen village is one of a string of fishing villages which face the shallow warm waters of the Straits of Taiwan. It was founded in the early seventeenth century by migrants from the area around the city of Amoy, Fukien province. Its size has been increased by later waves of migration from the same area and from other villages in southwestern Taiwan so that today it has over 3000 inhabitants. The villagers are all speakers of the Ch'uan-chou dialect of Hokkien. Physically they resemble the population of southeastern China, with perhaps some slight admixture with the indigenous aboriginal population.

In relation to its neighboring farming villages and to the city, K'un Shen is regarded as a poor community, engaged in occupations that have low prestige. In traditional Chinese thinking, the scholars/officials held the top ranks in society, followed by farmers, artisans, and merchants, in that order. Fishermen were usually thought to be in a class of "mean people" below the four respectable classes. They were often barred from taking the examinations that led to political office and privilege, and were looked down on by society. However, in terms of actual wealth and life style they were often no worse off than the average peasant who owned or rented a small amount of land. In many instances they might be much better off than the tenant farmer. Be that as it may, K'un Shen, together with other fishing villages, still shares to some degree in the traditional stigma attached to its sources of livelihood. The majority of its population depends on raft fishing, while others cultivate fish ponds, or operate as small merchants and traders, as artisans, service workers, and hired laborers, or engage in the small amount of farming that the land allows. The village elite are its merchants and pond owners. No true gentry class of landlords/scholars could develop here.

On an island like Taiwan fishing is, of course, an important source of income. Since the onset of Japanese colonial rule, modern fishing ports have developed and small coastal and inshore fisheries have been encouraged. Well over half-a-million people are at work in some branch of the fisheries industry. The coastal and in-shore fisheries yield a rich harvest of mackeral, mullet, sardine, bonito, and many other varieties, while pond cultivation provides a marketable supply of carp, oysters, shrimp, milkfish, and seaweeds to be used as condiments. Although the fishermen do not expect to become rich, they expect a comfortable living and enough cash to meet their needs.

The village of K'un Shen is easily reached from Tainan except during the heavy summer rains. Buses and bicycles follow a dirt road which winds southwest from the city, passes through a farming village, crosses numerous small bridges, and finally terminates 8 miles later in K'un Shen. As one enters the village, one sees houses lined along one side of the road and on the other side, scrub and dunes leading down to the sea. Tall trees flank the road, providing coolness and color.

As one follows any of the numerous alleys leading into the heart of the village, the greenery disappears. Here and there a tree has been left standing, its shade creating a natural gathering place, but for the most part, the eye sees brown dust, dull red brick, gray tile, and a jumble of one-story houses built close together in a random pattern. Save for one winding, semipaved road that circles the village, there are no laid-out streets. Traffic moves between houses via passageways and alleys that are often not wide enough for two persons to walk abreast. The alleys and road converge, eventually, on a large paved plaza, the length of a long city block. At its west end is the main temple of the village, with its bright multicolored roof. Along its north and south sides are the shops and stalls, which provide the village with foodstuffs, daily necessities, and a few services. There are two large general stores

The main square of the village, with shops and temple.

which sell rice, oil, canned goods, condiments, and the like, two barbershops, a bicycle repair shop, a noodle restaurant, two fruit stands, and a vegetable stall. During the morning hours there is an outdoor market; one can find peddlers of vegetables and fruits, the village butcher, fish sellers, and sometimes a peddler from the city with cloth or brooms or ready-made clothing, which he has precariously balanced on his bicycle.

The plaza is the center of the village and it is rarely empty except during the hot noon hours, when everyone rests. It is more than a marketplace. It is a playground for the children, a sunlit place to dry fish and sweet potatoes, a gathering place for religious festivals, village meetings, or casual socializing. At night it is as lively as during the day; there may be a traveling medicine show performing its acts there, or a dance group from the temple rehearsing, or a cluster of men discussing village affairs. On very hot summer nights, the men and boys often bring their sleeping mats along and sleep outside to take advantage of the ocean breezes.

Housing

The east end of the plaza terminates in fish ponds and a river inlet. The village houses spread out on the other three sides. Except for two new multistory dwellings, the village houses are built in traditional Chinese style, one-story high.

Red brick predominates, though some of the poorer families build with wood, bamboo, and plastered mud and some of the newest houses use concrete. Roofs are of a dark-gray tile, with bricks placed at intervals on top to hold them during typhoons. There is little outside decoration, though a few of the older houses have a row of painted ceramic tiles over the doorway or along the edge of the roof. A few houses have walls or spirit screens to hide the doorway from the view of passersby. Some have low walls which allow those inside to look out, or those outside to look in. Most have only a paved or earth courtyard fronting directly onto the street, with the house and its outbuildings built around three sides of the court. The heavy wooden doors at the front and back of the house are shut and bolted during the night, but during the daytime they stand open. Windows are barred for protection, but are rarely closed except during cold weather and storms.

The style of building gives little privacy, which is not really sought during the day. Much of the women's work is done outdoors. The courtyard or doorway is a work area for netweaving, food preparations, sewing, laundering, and the like. The kitchen is usually a semiopen shed at the side of the house proper, or a portable charcoal stove set in the courtyard or on the street. In the evenings, the courtyards are used for sponge baths, except in those few households that have wash houses.

The village has electricity, and most homes have at least one outlet. There are ten or so street lamps distributed through the village, illuminating gathering places and kept burning through the night. Shops and refreshment stands continue business until about 11:00 P.M., and activity resumes again in the early morning.

The onset of bad weather drives some activity into the houses, into the main or central room. The most common house plan is in the shape of a rectangle (see diagram). The doorway leads directly into the central room, with the sleeping rooms at right angles behind walls or partitions on either side of the central room. There is also a storage area running the length of the house behind the central room. If the family is fairly well off, additional sleeping rooms are added along the court at the front of the house. Sometimes a brick kitchen may be attached. The benjo (outhouse) is usually a separate structure at a distance from the house. Most families do not have a private benjo, but use the nearest public ones, of which there are many.

The central room serves many functions. It is a dining room, a playroom, a room for entertaining guests, a work area and storage area, at times an extra bedroom or a room where the dead lie in state awaiting burial. At all times it is a religious room. It holds the family's altar, a large carved table on which are placed the ancestral tablets or shrines and offerings of food and incense. The same altar also serves one or another of the Buddhist or Taoist gods that the family has selected as its special protector. Flowers, candles, wine cups, and plates of sweets are arrayed on the altar for the gods and ancestors. Over the altar hangs a picture of a dead parent or a painting or print of a deity, but the presence of an altar does not prevent secular activities from taking place or inhibit them in any way. Nor is the altar the only religious note in the room. The heavy front doors are usually painted with representations of fierce warriors who guard the household, and these are visible during the day from within the room when the doors are open.

Depending on the wealth of the family, the floors are of dirt or concrete, and the amount and quality of the furnishings vary. In poorer households the room

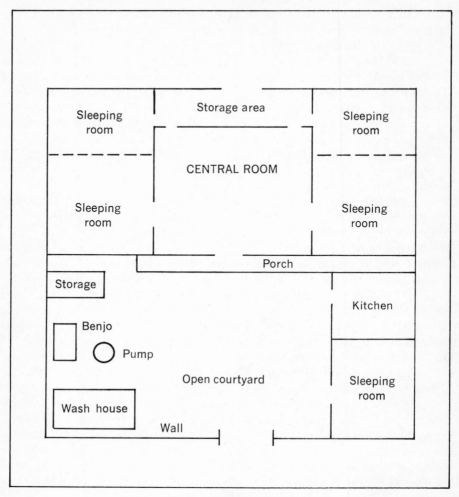

House plan for middle-income family.

is furnished with a few low bamboo stools, a wooden dining table, and pictures from magazines or a calendar decorating the walls. Fishing equipment and firewood are stored in the corners. In the wealthier families, the central room is more elaborately furnished. There are Western-style chairs with plastic upholstery, mirrors on which are painted nature scenes in unnatural colors, photographs of family members, a wall clock, and on the family altar, a brightly colored plastic radio. If the house is of recent vintage, or if a marriage has recently taken place, there are scrolls from family and friends bearing good wishes.

Guests in the home usually do not see more than this central room. The sleeping rooms are private areas, and usually simply furnished, no matter what the income level of the family. Few houses own bedsteads, the preference being for a raised platform some 2 feet high made of wood or stone. On this, mats or Japanese *tatami* are spread, to serve as a bed at night and a place to sit during the day. The platform takes up most of the room, running the entire width and half or more of the length. Wooden closets for storing quilts, clothing, and mosquito netting are usually placed on the platform itself. On the floor there will be a small mirrored vanity table holding the wife's cosmetics, and in a corner, a stand for a washbasin. In the bedrooms of younger couples one may now find a sewing machine, this being a popular dowry item.

Kitchen facilities are also simple. In the attached room or shed used as a kitchen there is a wooden table for chopping and cutting foods and a glass-doored or screened cabinet for storing dishes and leftover foods: this is sometimes kept in the central room. Some families have brick stoves fed with wood or charcoal, which can hold four pots at the same time. Others use portable charcoal burners, which hold only one pot. In some households the kitchen also serves as a dining room.

A few of the better-off families have washhouses within the compound. These hold a small tub, which is filled from buckets drawn at the well or pump. Others serve only as a private retreat for a sponge bath. Two families had Japanese-style *ofuro*: deep wooden tubs with a charcoal burner to heat the water. Most villagers, however, prefer to bathe in cold water.

Toilet facilities, whether public or private, are modeled after the Japanese *benjo*: an outhouse with a floor hole over which one squats or stands, and a door for privacy. Beneath the *benjo* is a deep pit. This is cleaned every 10 or 12 days, and the night soil is either sold or used as fertilizer in the fish ponds and fields by the owners. During the summer months, flies breed actively in the *benjos*. Nowadays most are treated with chemicals to cut down the number of maggots, not always successfully.

As in most other places in Taiwan, the sewage system is a series of open drains flowing along the sides of the lanes. Small children use the sewers as a latrine and some food garbage finds its way into the sewers as well. Most food leftovers and scraps are fed to the pigs and chickens, so that there is relatively little problem of garbage disposal. Paper waste is burned. Mainly, the sewers carry water from laundering and dishwashing. They drain into the canals and fish ponds surrounding the village.

Most village water comes from wells, of which there are some 27 scattered throughout the community. Eight of these are large public wells, the remainder smaller and semipublic. Twelve families have installed pumps in their courtyards. The local water is salty; even when it is boiled for a long time, a brackish taste remains. Women who grew up in other villages complain about it. The wells are a gathering place for the women of the village. It is their task to draw water in the early morning, and at midmorning they regroup to do their laundry around the wells, in company.

Clothing

Ordinary dress in K'un Shen reflects Japanese and Western influence. Adult males now favor khaki trousers or knee-length shorts for everyday work and wear.

Mornings, women congregate at a well to gossip and launder.

This is topped with a white T-shirt, though some of the men will go barechested in warm weather. Low-cost *zori* of rubber, or wooden clogs held by a plastic band across the toes, are common for both men and women, and many of the villagers go barefooted. On more formal occasions, the men wear a Western-style sports shirt or white shirt with khaki trousers or trousers of dark-colored wool or rayon, Only the very old men still wear the traditional Chinese costume: loose-fitting dark-blue trousers and matching long jacket. Most items of male dress are bought ready-made. In the winter months the men add leather and woolen jackets, heavy sweaters, or sweat shirts to their costume. On rainy days, most wear plastic raincoats in bright colors. A few still wear the traditional straw poncho.

Women's clothing also has shifted away from traditional dress, except for those women in their late fifties or older. Among these older women one still finds bound feet and Chinese costume—the loose-fitting long trousers and side-fastening jacket in dark blue, black, or white cotton or silk, and the hair combed into a tight bun high on the neck and held in place with gold ornaments. Most of the women, however, look to the Japanese-style books or effect a compromise between East and West in their dress. For everyday wear, the women prefer loose cotton skirts or loose trousers that fall a few inches below the knee, topped with a loose-fitting blouse. For dress, some wear the *ch'i-pau*, which is usually much longer and looser than those worn by the recent Mainland refugees. Others wear two-piece suit-dresses based on Japanese patterns. Women wear very little jewelry, except for rings and hair ornaments, and the latter are disappearing. Most women wear their hair short and a considerable number have had permanents, at least among the young and middle-aged women.

Both sexes wear palm-leaf sunhats at work, and except in poor families, the adult members wear large-sized men's watches as accessories. Clothing for both sexes tends to be muted in color, and items of dress are worn until they can no longer be patched and mended. Only the young people, the children, and the unmarrieds are seen in bright colors. Girls in their teens frequently wear brightly colored full skirts and blouses, or Western-style dresses bought with their earnings, and on holidays the children from the better-off families are dressed in reds and bright blues. Even the children's dress, however, tends to be drab most of the time. During the week they wear their khaki school uniforms, or faded garments handed down from older siblings or cousins. Following school regulations, the boys' hair must be shaved or clipped close, and girls are required to wear their hair in a straight "dutch bob," a style which now extends to the preschoolers as well. The school also discourages the children from going barefoot. If the family can afford it, children wear sneakers; otherwise, they wear wooden clogs or *zori*.

Diet and Food Preparation

There is little distinction made between the foods considered appropriate at the three daily meals. Most foods are considered suitable for all meals. What is left over from supper is served at breakfast, and rice and side dishes from breakfast may reappear at lunch. Breakfast is taken between 6:00 and 7:30 A.M., lunch during the noon hours, and dinner after sunset. The staple at each meal is rice, or rice mixed together with sweet potato, and augmented with small amounts of fish, vegetables, pickles, or sometimes pork and duck. Only the wealthiest families eat pure rice at every meal; in the poorest families rice is a luxury and sweet potato the staple.

Meals generally are frugal. As might be expected, most of the proteins in the diet come from fish: milkfish, sardine, carp, and various small fish which are caught in village waters, but have little market value. Fried oysters and shrimp also appear as part of ordinary fare. Meat is seldom served. Many families will not eat beef at all because of Buddhist restrictions against it. Technically, they should not eat pork either, but pork is the main meat used on feast days and mixed in small quantities with vegetables at ordinary meals. The fatter cuts of pork are preferred. From time to time bean curd, sausage, or salted fish appear at daily meals. Eggs are a luxury—in one fairly well-off family I knew, a fried egg was occasionally served and divided among three adults and two children.

There are many different fruits and vegetables available in the village, brought in by local peddlers or people from nearby communities. The village uses bamboo shoots, cabbage, cauliflower, cucumber, eggplant, green onions, leeks, sponge gourd, sprouts, string beans, and winter melon. The usual method of preparation is stir frying, or else boiling a vegetable together with a few scraps of pork, soy sauce, and vinegar to make a soup. Tomatoes are available in great quantity throughout the year, and are regarded as a fruit to be taken as a snack between meals. Other fruits, such as guavas, papayas, mangos, pineapples, and oranges, are also eaten as snacks.

In most families, the preparation of a dish is done in enough quantity that it can be served at one or two subsequent meals. Leftovers are rarely reheated, and most foods are served warm rather than hot. Hot foods are not considered healthy or tasty.

For holidays, the food preparations are more elaborate, and more expensive ingredients are used. The proportion of rice to sweet potato increases, and noodles cooked with pork or oysters are also used as a staple. A typical feast meal would include two or three dishes of vegetables mixed with pork or fish, a dish of fried fish, a dish of fatty pork or a duck, and a soup made with fish balls. The variety is greater than on ordinary days, particularly if the family is entertaining guests. Feasts also include rice wine or soda. The most elaborate feasts take place at weddings. Then, the family is expected to serve at least twelve different dishes to the guests, including true delicacies such as pigeons' eggs, cuttlefish, mushrooms, pig's stomach, and sharks' fins.

There is considerable eating of snacks between meals. One favorite is a spicy soup with lumps of coagulated pig's blood, sold each morning by a visiting peddler woman. Another woman sold a soup of sweet berries. In the winter months there is a stand selling hot bean-curd milk and peanut soup. The small restaurant near the temple offers a soup of beans and pork hocks at all hours of the day and night. In warmer weather people buy large slices of watermelon, bottled soda, ices, or stalks of sugarcane. Other available snacks include such things as betel nut, candies, pickled fruits, sweet rolls, peanuts, and cookies.

Liquor consumption is minimal. There is no wine shop in the village. The general stores sell several brands of rice wine, *kaoliang*, and medicinal wines, but these are used at home and only on special occasions. Other liquors appear from time to time on the store shelves and gather dust for months on end. These include rum, plum brandy, and a rough whiskey. The purchasers, for the most part, seem to be the retired Mainland soldiers settled in the village.

Tea drinking is also minimal. There is no tea shop in the village, and the saltiness of the village water discourages people from serving tea at home. On the rare occasions that tea is served, it is usually black tea of the cheapest grade. Bottled soda is preferred for guests.

Western foods such as condensed milk and a singularly tasteless instant oatmeal, sold in the village, are regarded as food for infants only. Even then, the use depends on the mother's milk supply. Sweet rolls and white bread are sometimes given to young children as between-meal snacks, but the adults considered them uninteresting.

┌─────┐
│ 2 │
└─────┘

The Economic Base
of Village Life

Occupational Distribution

T HE MAJORITY OF HOUSEHOLDS in K'un Shen are involved in sea fishing. Probably in no household is the only income from fishing, but for most households it is the major source of income, and most of the working force engages in it at least part time.

Because of the size of the community, it was not possible to get a detailed breakdown of occupation for all working members, but a rough idea can be gained from the occupational listings for one section of the village. The section had 146 households and a total population of 972 persons. Of these, 185 males and 146 females listed fishing as the major source of income; for the men this usually meant raft fishing, and for the women net hauling from the beach. Another 23 men (no women) were listed as having fish-pond cultivation as their major source of income; 35 men and 1 woman worked as fish sellers; 8 men and 9 women worked as merchants or peddlers; 3 men and 1 woman worked as farmers. Seventy-four adult women had no occupational listing other than housewife, though this does not preclude doing some part-time work. Only 8 women were listed as holding factory or shop jobs in the city, but this figure is less accurate; a sizeable number of unmarried girls now take low-paying factory jobs. There were also 6 men working as day laborers, 8 men holding various white-collar or professional jobs, and 14 holding factory jobs.

In reality, most families depend on the income from several jobs. A household that relies primarily on fishing, which brings in an average income of $600 NT a month in season, may also own a small plot of farmland for raising sweet potatoes, and the wife may earn extra cash by weaving hairnets or shucking oysters.[1]

---

[1] At the time of this study, the exchange rate was 40 New Taiwan dollars (NT) for $1 U.S. money.

11

Few in the younger generation desire to become raft fishermen, and instead look to the city as a source of new occupations. If they are apprenticed to factory jobs, they are already bringing in a small income while in their teens and relieving the household of the burden of their support.

Sea Fishing

The fishing season begins in the tenth lunar month (late November) and continues into the third or fourth lunar month. There is little fishing done during the summer, because of typhoons and unsuitable prevailing winds.

Fishing is done close to shore, usually within sight of land. On rough days the rafts do not venture out. The normal fishing day is from 4:00 or 5:00 A.M. until noon, although fishing sometimes continues until dark. In earlier days, the rafts often went out at night.

None of the rafts are mechanized. Power is provided by oars and sail. The rafts are of simple construction, and usually made by their owners, who also do the necessary repair work. Eight to twelve heavy bamboo poles are lashed together with rattan. The more poles used, the larger they are in size, with the length varying from 15 to 21 feet. Oarlocks are located at the bow and stern. There are also small rafts of four to seven poles in size, propelled by only one set of oars. These are used only on the river inlet or on the fish ponds.

The bamboos used are imported from the mountain regions and are brought to the village at the beginning of each season by city traders or by the local Fishermen's Association. The cost is high, ranging from $100 to $160 NT per pole, and poles must be replaced as they become worn and waterlogged. New poles are scraped of bark and then bent into a slightly curved shape by application of heat and stone weights. The bow end curves up sharply, rising a foot or more. The bending process takes at least a week of labor. Afterward, the poles are oiled and stained, a task that must be repeated at the beginning of each fishing season and once again midway through the season. The poles are dyed reddish brown with vegetable dye and heavily coated with tung-seed oil. This makes the poles waterproof, and less likely to crack or dry out.

The raft is then assembled, lashed together with rattan at nine or ten points. Thin pieces of bamboo are lashed across at the places where the oarlocks are attached. If the raft is to have a sail, a centerboard must be lashed to the base. The total cost of staining, oiling, and lashing is estimated at between $200 and $500 NT each time.

If the raft has a sail (and not all have), the owner buys white canvas from the city market and dyes it with pig's blood, betel juice, or the same dye used on the poles. This costs about $200 NT. Oars are commissioned from carpenters in the city, at a cost of about $150 NT per pair. Rafts also have miscellaneous equipment such as baskets, straw matting, and lanterns. The cost of building and maintaining a raft is considerable, the initial outlay being the equivalent of three or four months' income, and the cost of yearly upkeep amounting to about a half month's income.

We have not yet considered the expense of the fishing equipment itself. There are a variety of nets in use in the village. The most common is a nylon-mesh net, which can be used for a variety of fish: mullet, hairtail, mackerel, carp, *shitao,* sole, plaice, bonito, and even sardine and anchovy. These nets have been made available through the Fishermen's Association and have been quickly accepted because of their lightness, durability, and versatility. The cost ranges from $5000 to $10,000 NT, depending on size. These are used by single rafts or two rafts working together.

More traditional equipment is also in use. The most elaborate and expensive nets are the beach-seining nets for catching sardine and anchovy. In dried form these fish are one of the staples of the Taiwanese diet and find a ready market in Japan. There are three such nets still in use in the village. They are made of heavy cotton or hemp mesh in 12 sections. The net, when put together, is semicircular in shape and about 900 feet in length. At two sides, another 900 feet of rope are attached for hauling. The net terminates in a pouch 48 feet long.

During the winter months, these nets are in use through the daylight hours. A large working force is required—at least 50 persons hauling from the beach, and another 5 persons on a raft spreading the net on the water. Pulling in the net takes about two hours each time. Men, women, and children all participate in the work, the men working near the water or immersed to their waists in water, and the women and children farther up the beach pulling and coiling the rope as it comes in. The work is done in relative silence. There is no singing or chanting; only subdued conversation. As the pouch is drawn in, there is a rise in voices and excitement, with people talking and joking, wading out into the water and crowding around to see what the net holds.

With average luck, the catch during the three-month season will be worth around $16,000 NT. Of this, 40 percent goes to the owner of the net and rafts, and the remainder is apportioned out to the haulers and boatmen on a share basis. The boatmen get six shares each, able-bodied men get four shares, women and children get two shares or less. Miscellaneous fish that turn up in the net, plus a handful or two of the catch, are given to the hauling crew.

Another specialized net is used for mullet. The season is limited to the ten days preceding and following the winter solstice. In the past, mullet were an important source of income for the village, but recently the fish schools have been declining, due to the increased activities of Chinese and Japanese trawlers and motorized craft and changing water temperatures and weather conditions.

In mullet fishing, four rafts encircle the school of fish, while a fifth raft enters the circle and drives the mullet into pockets at the base of the net. The nets are made of a heavy cotton fiber or hemp, and are about 525 feet long and 40 feet high. Bamboo floats ring the top edge, and the base pockets are spaced about 2 feet apart.

During the short season, the mullet fishermen eat, sleep, and rest in brush and bamboo huts on the beach so that they can be on call when a school is sighted. One man is hired solely to cook for them, and the net owners are expected to provide rice, oil, fuel, wine, and a number of side dishes for them. At night, the workers may visit their homes, but are expected to return to the hut to sleep. Staying at the hut is tied to beliefs about good luck in fishing. It is believed that the workers will be visited in their dreams by spirits who give information about the location of a school or who will wake them when the fish are running in village waters.

Many religious beliefs and practices are tied to mullet fishing. Each hut flies

Mending nylon nets.

Drying nylon nets at the end of the work day. Note more traditional hemp net drying behind the woman.

a black flag in front of it; this is insurance against angry spirits who died in accidents at sea and may still haunt the beach. Inside each hut is an altar on which wooden figures or scrolls bearing the names of different gods are kept. If the god has a shaman, he will give advice on location and time for successful fishing. In addition, the fishermen visit one or another of the small shrines located near the beach to burn incense and ask for protection and good luck during the season.

Traditionally, the owner of the boats and nets receives 40% of the profits and the work crew receives shares of the remainder. However, some of the mullet-fishing groups are complex cooperatives or partnerships. For example, one group had 4 net owners, one of whom also owned a raft. There were 4 others who each owned a raft. These owners worked as a part of the crew together with relatives or friends aiding them. The total profits were divided into 25 shares: 1 share to each of the 15 members of the group, half a share to each man who owned a raft, one-and-a-half shares to each man owning a section of the net, and one-and-a-half shares to the owner of the raft which worked within the encirclement.

During previous seasons, the value of the mullet catch per crew averaged $50,000 NT. The flesh of the fish alone is prized, and at this winter season the mullet are also heavy with roe, an expensive delicacy. Today, however, the value of the catch is considerably less. Whereas a member of the work crew might once have earned $2000 NT for the three-week period, he is now lucky to earn $500 NT.

The encirclement method used for mullet is also used for catching sardines, with two to four rafts cooperating and using smaller nets. Sea bass, mackerel, and bonito are sometimes caught in the same fashion.

Dragnetting is also done from rafts. Two rafts work together to pull a net about 260 feet long made of heavy hemp fiber. The last 60 feet of the net form a pouch in which the fish are trapped. Dragnetting is used for a variety of fish: anchovy, *shitao,* sardine, bonito, and other species of mullet. On good days, the group earns up to $200 NT in this work. Formerly, dragnetting for sea bass was done at night, but government restrictions now make this impossible.

All of the forms of fishing described so far involve cooperation between two or more rafts or groups of workers. Rafts belonging to related households frequently work together for short periods, and friends cooperate in similar fashion. However, much of the fishing time is used in greater isolation: a single raft with two or perhaps three men equipped with nylon throw nets. There is also hook fishing, using long nylon wire with multiple hooks baited with shrimp or tiny fish. Mackerel and various flatfish can be caught in this manner. The rafts bob on the water, waiting three or four hours before drawing in the line. There is also crab netting during the winter months. Mesh baskets with a crisscross of bamboo over the top are let down by ropes, and the crabs trapped inside. Mesh baskets are also used to catch shrimp, eel, and crab in the river inlet. Basket trapping brings in only a small income.

The fishermen keep a part of the catch for household use, but most of it is sold through the government-sponsored Fishermen's Association, whose office is located on the beach. The fish are weighed there and spread on a concrete floor for examination. Dealers from the village or from the city bid on them. The Association takes 4% of the price as its fee and keeps track of the sales each fisherman makes. After the fish are sold, they are loaded into baskets, which are placed on the backs of bicycles and taken into the city. There are no refrigeration facilities in the village, so there is pressure for the boats to put in by noon, when the largest number of fish dealers are waiting to make their purchases.

Despite the quantity of fish that are caught, the more valuable ones rarely find their way onto village dining tables. Bream, carp, mullet, and mackerel are regarded as luxury foods and eaten only rarely. The fisherman's household eats mainly the small fish that have low market prices.

In addition to providing marketing facilities, the Fishermen's Association functions as an educational organization. During the slack summer months it holds training classes. Films and lectures are presented which describe methods of fishing from motorized vessels and deep-sea craft. Many village fishermen are aware of the advantages of mechanization, but local conditions have made it impossible to adopt many of the new methods. Unlike many neighboring villages, K'un Shen has no natural harbor and the rafts must be beached. If a man were to invest in a motorized boat, he would be faced with problems of anchorage, particularly during the typhoon season. Boats do not have free access to existing coastal harbors. Special military permits are needed to enter or leave, so that boats cannot run for shelter to the nearest harbor when a storm rises. Thus, the changes that have been adopted are minimal. Except for the increasing use of nylon general-purpose nets, the past few decades have not brought any changes in fishing techniques and technology.

Pond Cultivation

Many households own fish ponds and derive a major or secondary portion of their income from them. The village ponds are specialized for breeding milkfish, silver carp, grass carp, mouthbreeders, oysters, and prawns. The industry was already well established when the Japanese arrived.

The oyster ponds are located along the river inlet where the water mixes with salt water at high tides. Much of this area is owned by the village temple, which collects rent from the users. The produce can be sold by user without going through the Fishermen's Association, and much of it is sold within the village proper and kept for home use.

Caring for an oyster pond requires some four to eight hours of work each day. The average pond produces about 400 catties of oysters each year, and the market price per catty is around $20 NT.[2] Most of the profit goes to the owner, who needs to hire additional labor only when the oysters are being "harvested." Then, he hires village women and children to shuck the oysters, paying them $0.50 NT per catty of shucked oysters. A fast worker can make $10 NT a day, and it is a valued source of additional income for the poorer village households.

To the north and south the village is bordered with freshwater ponds fed by streams and irrigation channels. These are used for raising silver carp and grass carp. The same pond is used for both species; the silver carp are scavangers which

---

[2] A catty is 1⅓ pounds.

keep the pond clean. Since grass carp will not breed in ponds, the fry must be purchased from outside sources. Most are originally imported from Hong Kong or the Philippines. Silver-carp fry cost $1 NT each, and the price of grass carp fry varies from $.80 to $ 2 NT in different years. It takes a year or more for the fry to grow to eating size, when they sell for $50 or $60 NT each.

Labor on the ponds continues through the year. They must be cleaned periodically, particularly after heavy rains, when mud washes down from the sides. In winter, it is necessary to build bamboo and straw windbreaks to protect the fish. Foodstuffs must be carried out to the ponds every day: duckweed, grass, cabbage, rice bran, and peanut husks. Night soil is also added to the ponds to encourage plant and insect growth for the fish to feed on. Owners estimate that they spend from four to six hours daily working on their ponds, and often extra labor is hired.

The majority of village ponds are given over to milkfish. The fry are sometimes purchased, sometimes caught in the shallow waters of the sea and river in April and May. They are extremely sensitive—only about 20 percent survive in the ponds. They are affected adversely by cold, or by an imbalance in the amounts of fresh and salt water brought into the ponds. After a year, they are large enough to eat, averaging four to five per catty. After another 4 months they reach a maximum size of 1 catty in weight. The half-grown fish sell for between $.60 and $1.60 NT per catty; full-grown milkfish will bring $6.00 NT per catty on the market. An average pond used for raising milkfish is capable of producing a yearly income of $15,000 NT or more if used for growing the fish to their full size. For raising carp, an average pond will hold 600 grown fish comfortably, bringing in an income well over $30,000 NT every 14 or 15 months.

A few ponds are used for raising shrimp and prawns, with fry caught in the shallow waters and river. They are difficult to raise, and if water conditions are not right, as, for example, after a heavy rain, there may be a total loss. However, it is a profitable venture if they survive. Prawn sell for $80 NT per catty at full growth and for about $45 NT when small. Few households are willing to take the gamble; most of the prawn and shrimp are raised by families who have other ponds for raising fish. In one small pond they will try to raise 1000 prawn or about 10,000 shrimp. If they fail, there are other resources to fall back on.

Another use for the ponds is to turn them over to the raising of seaweed, which is used in making agar or as a food in itself. An initial investment of about $55 NT will return a profit of $500 NT in two months. Often, K'un Shen is redolent with the smell of dying seaweed. The plants are spread across the temple square, in courtyards, and on the sunbaked road and streets. During the Japanese period, great quantities were grown because of the demands of the Japanese market, and many buyers would come out to the village to bid. The demand has lessened in recent years.

The Fishermen's Association is not concerned with the fish-pond industry. Sales of pond produce are made directly to dealers based in the village or city. Some pond owners themselves transport the fish to companies in the city and put them up for auction to bidders from other parts of Taiwan.

Most pond-owning households are wealthier than fishermen's households. Much depends on weather and water conditions, as well as the size of the pond.

Even with the uncertainties, however, many pond owners are in the middle- or upper-income strata of village life and can rely solely on the ponds for a comfortable income.

Farming and Animal Husbandry

Very few village families are full-time farmers. Most of the farming done by village families is limited to sweet potatoes and brushwood used as fuel, both of which are for household consumption.

The landholdings are small. The average plot is only sufficient for growing 4000 sweet potatoes. Planting is done during the seventh and eighth lunar months, and the harvest comes in the second and third lunar months following. The field is then turned over to brush, which is harvested in the seventh lunar month. The cycle is then repeated.

Pig manure and night soil are used as fertilizer, with some purchase of chemical fertilizer. The fields are prepared with a plough. There are three draft oxen owned by villagers and they are rented out at $45 NT a day. The ploughing of a plot can be done in a day or a day and a half. Ploughing is always done by men.

The rest of the agricultural work can be done by either men or women. The tasks of weeding, transplanting, and harvesting are suitable to either sex, and in practice much of the work is left to the women since the men are busy with other jobs. Once the sweet potatoes are harvested, the women shred them into strips and

A woman and her daughter-in-law shred sweet potatoes for drying.

lay them to dry in the sun to preserve them for year-round use. Harvesting of the brushwood also is mainly a woman's task. The oldsters and children help her to break it up and bind it into bundles.

All families who own farmland are eligible for membership in the Farmers' Association, a government-sponsored organization parallel to the Fishermen's Association. It has loan facilities, occasionally shows training films, and distributes a monthly magazine. Recently, it has been encouraging the villagers to try growing hemp or peanuts.

Most village families raise a few animals for home use or sale. Chickens are by far the most common: almost every household owns a few. During the day, they run freely around the courtyards and streets and through the houses foraging for food. Ducks, geese, and turkeys are also raised in the village. The eggs from the various poultry are usually sold to one of the village stores and from there, to the city.

At least 25 households in the village raise pigs, which they sell to the village butcher or to the Tainan market. The pigs are kept in pens near the house and are fed on sweet potato, table scraps, and milk powder obtained through aid programs.

There are no dairy animals in the village except for the draft oxen, which function only as work animals. Other animals are rare. Some of the young boys in the newly formed 4-H Club raise rabbits. Few households have dogs: they are not regarded as desirable pets, and there is no need for watchdogs in K'un Shen. There are also a number of cats, but it is difficult to assess how many because they are semiwild and rarely can tolerate being in the presence of humans.

Traders, Merchants, and Urban Workers

Trade of various kinds is an important source of income to village families. About 14% of household heads are classified as merchants in the official records and many other persons engage in trade on a part-time basis. There are at least three different kinds of merchants: those who own shops in the village, those who work in the fish trade between village and city, and peddlers. The village has many stores: two large general stores, four small general stores, four barbershops, a drugstore, a bicycle repair shop, three restaurants, two pool halls, at least four permanent stands which sell ices, fruit, and soda, and two permanent stands which sell vegetables and fruit. During the day, peddlers move from place to place selling candies, hot soups, ice creams, household sundries, fried buns, fruits and vegetables, cloth, and other items. Many of the younger village men are engaged in the fish trade.

The two largest general stores have capital investments of about $100,000 NT and the smaller ones between $2500 and $10,000 NT. They sell a wide variety of items, from rice and soy sauce for daily use to firecrackers and wine for special occasions.

The general stores open around 6:00 or 7:00 A.M. and do not shut their doors until midnight. Family members take turns waiting on the customers. Often, the owner's wife is in charge while her husband is away making purchases or looking after some other business. The children of the family help in the store after school, and study there in between serving the customers. The general stores serve as meeting places for village men, who congregate there in the evenings to discuss fishing, listen to the news on the radio, or have someone read the newspaper to them.

The fresh-produce stands are simple affairs attached to houses located on the square. The income from them provides only a part of the owner's household income. Similarly, the stands selling fruits, soda, snacks, and ices generally do not provide a complete income for a household. Often, these stands are tended by the women and children, while the men do other work. Sometimes a household sells sugarcane or tomatoes in season, or has a small stock of betel nuts or candies which are sold from a table outside the doorway.

The number of village peddlers is hard to assess, since some work only part of the year. Moreover, there are nonresident peddlers who make the circuit of neighboring villages, selling brooms and brushes, pots, cloth, patent medicines, children's clothing, and picture books. Operators of games and novelty stands appear at festival times. Those peddlers native to the village are, for the most, women bringing in additional income to their households. They walk into Tainan early in the morning, buy produce, and return with their baskets on the early bus. Then they go from house to house vending their wares, usually earning about $10 NT a day. A few of the women peddlers work at selling sundries such as soap, cosmetics, needles, and thread.

There are a few skilled workers or artisans present in the village. One home has been transformed into a carpenter's shop, making chairs, tables, and cabinets for sale in the village and city. Another villager works part-time making paper houses for funerals, and paper figurines for religious ceremonies. A few of the young wives with sewing machines make clothing for other villagers, and many women earn a little cash weaving hairnets on consignment for a city broker. During the Japanese period, many of the women earned money sewing sacks for transporting sugar, but this home industry has died out as has weaving of fishing nets.

There are also a few members of the professions working in the village—two trained resident midwives, a doctor trained in Western medicine who operates an afternoon clinic, and the village druggist.

For the younger generation, the prospect of finding a job in the city holds more allure than the prospect of being a raft fisherman, and with increasing education and increasing industrialization the possibilities of this happening are much improved. There has always been some drain-off to the city, of course. Poor families with too many daughters used to send them off as servants or sell them into prostitution. During the slack season, men have always sought jobs as day laborers, but now there are new jobs, and a young person with primary schooling or, better still, a few years of middle-school training, has different options. Many hope for factory jobs and apprenticeships, or for white-collar positions. There are relatively few among the boys who aspire to be fishermen, and few girls expect to do nothing but help around the house prior to marriage. Many of the young will find work in the city. There is a demand for young workers, and the village is close enough to make commuting on a daily basis possible.

There is willingness by the parents to go along with this new trend. More and more, families feel the need for a cash income. The teen-age boys are not considered old enough to work on the rafts and would spend their adolescent years making little contribution to the family income except for the chance of finding a well-paying and permanent job in the city. Thus, parents are amenable to letting the boys become apprentices or factory workers. Some do not think of it as a permanent vocation, hoping that when the boy gets older he will find work in the village. The real objection, of course, is not the work itself, but the danger that the city worker will decide it is more convenient to make his residence in the city. Once this happens, ties and obligations to parents are loosened.

For the girls, work is only temporary; they do not expect to continue in their jobs after marriage. Meantime, they can work to bring in a cash income which in turn will enable them to marry with an impressive dowry. Most prestige items for dowries can only be obtained with cash, and the girl who works during her teens has the chance of making a better marriage.

However, most of the available city jobs are low-paying, except for some white-collar jobs in government offices which are open to middle-school graduates. The apprentice positions in shops and factories provide an average of $250 NT a month plus meals while working, and sometimes a place to sleep during the week. Regular factory workers make $600 NT a month. Pay for women runs lower than pay for men in comparable positions.

Village Class Structure

Having described briefly the occupations held by the people of K'un Shen, a few words should be said about the ranking of these occupations and the Confucian ranking of classes and occupations in traditional times. There is a four-class division into scholars/officials, farmers, artisans, and merchants found in the classical writings, and a parallel division of society into three broad classes of *shen-shih* (gentry), the *lao-pai-hsing* (common people) and the *chien-jen* (mean people). The *shen-shih* was the class of landowners-scholars-officials who held political as well as economic power, and the *lao-pai-hsing* included not only peasants, artisans, and merchants but also various others such as geomancers, fortune-tellers, and physiognomists, some musicians, painters, and also Taoist and Buddhist monks. The *chien-jen* held the despised occupations: actors, prostitutes, barbers and masseurs, servants, gravediggers, and shamans. Members of these groups were forbidden to intermarry with the two higher divisions and were barred from taking the official examinations.

In Taiwan, fishermen were regarded as *lao-pai-hsing*, although on the Mainland they were usually among the *chien-jen*. However, their general poverty and their noninvolvement in agriculture gave them a continuing low status in the eyes of other members of Taiwanese society. Households involved in fish-pond cultivation hold a higher status, but this is mainly within the social world of the fishing villages and not transferable to the society as a whole. Marriages are contracted between families of equivalent status within the circle of fishing villages. A family of wealthy pond owners equals another family of wealthy pond owners, not a wealthy farming household.

Within K'un Shen, the lines between classes are not rigidly fixed, but they are undeniably there. Income, education, and line of work combine to place a household somewhere within a hierarchy. The present ranking of occupations is, of course, not a traditional one, reflecting as it does the general culture-change situation, but it raises questions about the traditional ranking, particularly the status of the merchant and the peasant.

The modern educational system introduced by the Japanese probably had some influence on the present-day class hierarchy. During the Ch'ing dynasty, no member of the village had a classical education sufficient to allow him to win academic titles and government positions. However, under the Japanese some of the village children were educated, particularly the sons and daughters of the merchant and pond-owner families. As colonial rulers, the Japanese were the highest group in the village. Below them came sons of the village elite families who had been educated and became teachers and holders of minor government posts within the colonial administration. This was still in harmony with the traditional Chinese system. New upper-status roles also emerged during this period: the doctor of Western medicine, or the trained midwife, for example.

Today, K'un Shen's upper class is composed of storekeepers, pond owners, medical practitioners trained in either Chinese or Western medicine (including herb druggists), midwives, and government workers. Teachers are also a part of this group, but the villagers are reluctant to extend high status to the young people recruited to teach in the village school. K'un Shen's "middleclass," if looked at objectively, is "working class": skilled workers such as carpenters or tailors, providers of services such as barbers, peddlers, pedicab drivers, and factory hands. There is no romanticization of the role of the farmer, who is outranked by Taoist priests, by butchers and barbers, and by other occupations which technically should be listed in the lowest group by traditional standards. The occupations in which most villagers are involved come in the lowest group: fishermen, net haulers, day laborers, and part-time or small-scale peddlers.

Even at the village level, class affiliation is a crucial factor for selecting political leaders. They are almost always drawn from the upper class of pond owners, net owners, and other propertied families. They have sufficient funds to run a campaign and the leisure to carry out the duties of office, as well as the requisite education. The average person would not be able to keep the necessary records, write letters and draw up documents, or communicate as easily with the city officials.

Loan and Credit Facilities

No matter what economic class a household belongs to, there are times when it becomes necessary to borrow money, either as a support in some business enterprise or in order to tide the household over a crisis. Whatever the reason, it is considered important that the household obtain outside funds without becoming too dependent on the lender. For this reason, there is resistance to the idea of approaching kinsmen for loans, a fear that the household may lose its autonomy by putting itself in debt to a related household.

Although loans are available through the Fishermen's and Farmers' associations, the most favored source still is the private individual. There are at least ten persons in K'un Shen itself who serve as money lenders, including store owners, pond owners, a cloth merchant, and a barber. Loans are made at 3% interest per month or take the form of advance of credit at the stores. The store owners feel that if they do not extend credit, they will not be able to maintain their shops. There is no interest required, and they press for payment only at New Year's time. The pond owners often lend money to one another or to those who deal in fish fry, and take payment in kind rather than a return of cash.

Another way of obtaining money is through membership in a privately organized loan association of 10 to 20 friends. Loans are made on a rotating basis. Those recruited to such a club must be financially reliable, with the result that the poorer members of the community usually are not invited to participate.

Loans may also be obtained through the lineages. Several have loan funds which are made available at the time of the festivals held for the lineage patron god. The custom seems to be recent and began shortly after World War II as a means of paying festival expenses. Rather than continue asking the lineage members for donations at each festival, it was decided that the wealthiest families would contribute to a general fund to be lent out at 3% interest. The largest loan fund began with $2000 NT and has now reached $7000 NT. The increase derives not only from interest on loans but also from a secondary source. At each festival, households take home (and consume) turtle-shaped cakes of sugar and flour paste. The cakes are expected to insure safety, harmony, and prosperity for the household dur-

Inside the temple, lineage leaders reckon accounts and offer paste turtles for sale to bring luck to member households.

ing the year. Should the family pass the year without untoward incidents, they will return the same-sized cake or an equivalent sum of money, with a small amount of interest, in the following year. If it was a bad year, no interest is required. If the year that has passed is exceptionally good, then amount of interest must be commensurate with the benefits received. The amount of interest due is assessed in relation to the economic standing of the borrower household, and its success and failures during the year.

Out of the accumulating interest and repayments, money is available for small new loans which the borrower can repay with interest in a year. There is no question of confiscation of property or calling in outside agents to make good a debt, as often happens with loans received through the Fishermen's Association. Group pressure and the religious context of the transaction are usually sufficient to assure a return of the money within a reasonable time period. Borrowing from the lineage requires a guarantor from within the group, even though all are kinsmen. The transaction is thus put on a more impersonal basis. It is not the same as borrowing from relatives.

People hesitate to borrow from individual relatives, partly because of fear that it gives the other person control over them and partly because they fear loss of face should the loan be refused. There is a strong possibility that it will be refused, because on the lender's side is the fear that the loan will not be repaid or will be repaid very slowly. Moreover, it is embarassing to ask a kinsman to pay interest. If a man has surplus funds, he finds it more profitable to lend to nonkinsmen. There is some casual borrowing between kin. Married sisters willingly lend money to each other, or lend and borrow amongst their brothers, but brothers living in separate households avoid borrowing money from each other. Mothers and their grown children make loans to one another, but sons who are independently domiciled feel awkward about approaching their fathers for loans. Sisters-in-law, if they are on good terms, make small loans to each other to meet household expenses—this is one way of getting around the hesitancy of brothers to approach each other for loans. Kinsmen outside of the immediate family are rarely approached.

To quote several informants on the subject:

A mean-hearted man would certainly consider going to his brothers or relatives for help. This way he can save the interest.
Rely on yourself for everything and don't depend on your relatives. If you can't borrow from friends, and you borrow from your relatives, they will look down on you.
You have to plan things yourself, borrow money as capital and pay the interest to the lender. This way you'll feel easier about it. Some people like to get help from their relatives, and other people regard them unfavorably. He [that is, the borrower] just feels "it doesn't matter." Such people aren't strong-minded. I can't stand them.

Some people do borrow from relatives, judging from the remarks that are made on the subject, but a man has more face in the community if he is trusted by nonkinsmen in a business transaction and if he meets his obligations there.

Most villagers assert that their source of loans is friends and neighbors. Sometimes this means close friends, people with whom they have work ties and social ties, but often the word is used loosely, referring to acquaintances of a higher social class from whom they can borrow, or acquaintances in lines of work where there is a more ready supply of cash. Local fish dealers, for example, even though they do not have large supplies of cash that would enable them to be true money lenders, have enough to make small loans to the village fishermen. Some of the peddlers also make small loans to their customers. The relationship between borrower and lender is closer than between the city-based professional money lender and his clients; it mixes friendship and business ties.

Most people in K'un Shen are too poor to have much money to lend out, but one of the criteria for friendship seems to be the willingness to extend financial aid without thought of profit to oneself. Any profit that exists is indirect; the borrower has the reciprocal obligation to loan money at some future date. If this is understood and accepted by both parties, there is little shame and hesitancy in approaching a friend for a loan. In a close friendship, there may be no hesitancy at all. Sworn brothers often help each other with small loans, and women who are close friends frequently lend each other small sums of money from day to day. Usually, these are small loans. Fishermen turning to other fishermen borrow $30 or $40 NT at a time. Pond owners borrowing from each other may borrow $1000 NT at a time.

Environmental Control and Social Change

The various occupations—sea fishing, pond cultivation, and trading—involve some religious ritual as a necessary adjunct to practical experience, knowledge, and skills in order to achieve success. However, this should not be interpreted to mean that the villagers conceive of the ritual aspect as the crucial factor. Success is just more likely if certain ritual forms are observed. Ritual is sometimes carried out with a considerable degree of skepticism, but carried out nonetheless. Most often, it takes the form of thanking the supernatural world for benefits received or for protection from mishaps; only rarely is it ritual that asks for something to happen in the future.

For example, fish-pond owners are expected to perform a ceremony once a year to thank the god who protects the ponds and farms, *Lau-thi-kong*. Usually, only the male head of the household is present at the ceremony. He takes food offerings, incense, paper money, seven cups of wine, and seven pairs of chopsticks to the site of his pond and offers them there to the god. In the evening, the feast is consumed by the pond owner and invited friends.

On the fourteenth of the seventh lunar month, and at one or two other times during the year on the midpoint or last day of the month, pond owners will hold a ceremony for the "good brothers," a form of wandering ghost without descendants, to make food offerings to them. It is believed that these spirits become harmful if they are not fed and provided with money, wine, or incense. The ceremonies have as their objective persuading the spirits to withhold their potential to harm people and thanking them for withholding that power.

In similar fashion, merchant households hold ceremonies for the "good brothers" in the courtyards of their homes, thanking them for the profits and smooth operation of their businesses during the past months. Fishermen involved in mullet fishing and beach-seining operations also give thanks to the "good brothers" at the end of the fishing season, that is, at the end of the fourth lunar month. It is mainly the net owners who attend. Families who raise pigs for market, at the point where the negotiations for sale have been completed, will hold a ceremony to thank *Ti-tiau-kong* for allowing the pig to grow. A pig's head is offered to the god in addition to the more usual offerings of rice, wine, incense, and paper money. After the sale is completed, a second and similar ceremony is held. During the course of the year, most of the fishermen's families visit the *U-ieng-kong* shrines to present thanks offerings for the benefits received during the fishing season. Most commonly this is done at *Ch'ing Ming,* which is always celebrated on the third of the third lunar month, unlike other areas of China. Thanks are also offered during the seventh lunar month. The shrines to *U-ieng-kong* will be discussed more thoroughly in the chapter on religion. However, we may note that they are built to house the bones of persons unknown or without descendants to make offerings to them. They are thus potentially malevolent spirits who could do harm unless placated. The ceremonies at their shrines thank them for not doing, rather than for what they do, as a parallel to the ceremonies for the "good brothers."

In former years, when mullet fishing was more profitable, it was customary to hold a feast at the end of the mullet season. A pig was slaughtered, an opera troupe was invited to perform, and friends of the net owners and of the crew were invited to eat and drink. Offerings were made to the gods housed in the beach huts, thanking them for their help during the season. However, this practice has been curtailed by the decline in mullet fishing. Nowadays, the ceremony consists only of making small offerings of incense, paper money, and some foods at the altar tables and in the *U-ieng-kong* temples near the beach.

Observances for gods and spirits specifically connected with sea fishing continue in the present. Owners of fishing nets are expected to make food offerings to *Hai-lieng-ong*, the Sea King, at New Year, *Ch'ing Ming*, and the winter solstice. These ceremonies assure the protection of the boats and make the god amenable to helping the fishermen catch more fish. If a turtle is caught in the nets, another ceremony must be held to the Sea King so that he will not be offended and use his powers against the fishermen. The turtle is ceremoniously released back into the sea and paper money, incense, and firecrackers are offered to the god. Some fishermen believe that when the boats are in danger, the turtle (that is, the god in one of his forms) swims underneath the boat and helps carry it back to the shore.

There are other gods worshipped in the village who are related to fishing; none of them are gods kept in the larger village temples. In the several small-scale shrines located near the beach there are strips of paper bearing the names of gods who are believed to look after the welfare of fishermen. During the fishing season, incense is kept burning there, and after a particularly good day, a fisherman goes to offer incense and thanks at one of these small shrines. At New Years time, it is customary for the owners of fishing rafts to bring incense to the beach and plant it in the sand in front of their raft as a gesture of thanks. However, there are no religious artifacts carried on the rafts during working hours, and no religious rites involved in the building or refurbishing of a raft.

From the preceding data, it is obvious that religious elements are present in the economic sphere. At the same time man's role is seen as important in determining the degree of success. Natural explanations are often invoked to explain certain successes and failures. There is a great deal of "fishing knowledge": what seasons are appropriate, what depths of water, what kinds of currents, what times of day, what kinds of nets or lines to be used. In fish-pond cultivation, there are also many factors to consider: the salinity of the water, the depths of the pond, the kinds of feed, the rainfall, the temperature. If a man takes cognizance of these and plans his activities accordingly, he has some measure of control. If he chooses to ignore them or is careless, he fails—the gods have nothing to do with it. Although fishing and pond cultivation are both occupations which contain a high degree of risk, failure is not automatically assigned to supernatural causes. It may have human or natural causes.

The concept of "fate" or "fortune" is sometimes invoked as a last-cause explanation when failure cannot be attributed to natural causes alone or to lack of effort and skill by the individual. Women are more likely to use fate as an explanation than are men.

> A person's fate is most important. When a person meets with bad fortune, then no matter what he does its no use. . . . If a person has reached the time to die, no matter what medicines you use, there is no way to save him. If its not the time for him to die, if you just give him mud to eat he will get well.

According to this view, a person's undertakings may fail not through lack of action on his part or the part of others, but simply as a working out of fortune. Villagers disagree however, about when to blame fortune. A typhoon, a flood, a sudden frost whose effects are felt by everyone for miles around cannot by taken as evidence of individual fortune following a preordained path. These are natural events:

> For example, if there's a frost, its something nobody expects. With this sort of thing, you just have to bear with it.

As for the gods, they themselves are viewed as unreliable and capricious. To quote one informant:

> The gods are not always together with man. Sometimes they will leave man, like parents or elder sisters. They can't be together with us forever. A person runs in front of the gods, he bows to them for a long time, and nobody knows whether or not the gods come as a result. So I don't have any expectations about asking the gods for things.

In K'un Shen's view of things man must often depend on his own efforts and resources. Sometimes these are sufficient for the task. Other times they are not, and then one must simply bear with what is. Many villagers put stress on the importance of gaining knowledge and working hard. Some take the position that both man and the gods play roles in the economic sphere, but as man's knowledge increases, the role of the gods decreases. Said one informant:

Everything in the world depends half on heaven's help and half on man's researches. We can't say there are no gods. The weather depends on *Thi-kong's* actions. Sometimes the crops need rain. If it doesn't rain, the crops certainly can't grow. Regarding this kind of weather change, people must increase their research. All things in the world depend on what man's brain can think of, on man's ways of doing things.

If we summarize the body of beliefs discussed in the past few pages, the result would in part contradict itself, but the presence of contradictions does not negate the reality of the system in the minds of the villagers. Few bodies of thought are internally consistent—these villagers, like people in many other places in the world, have a choice of explanations and beliefs for different situations. In the economic sphere, there is recognition of the idea that the supernatural world influences and somehow controls the natural world and man's successes and failures therein. Running counter to this is the feeling that many events have natural or human causes and that one cannot assume the continual intervention of the supernatural into human affairs. Also, there is the conception of the supernatural as a negative rather than positive force. The "good brothers" are thanked for their nonintervention, and so are the spirits of the *U-ieng-kong* shrines. To the villagers, it is not at all clear whether or not particular gods associated with fishing actually do protect people from mishap or work positively to aid them in their endeavors. Ceremonies are often conducted for them because it seems to be the wisest course, something performed "just in case." Some people feel that ritual and morality in everyday life will encourage the supernatural world to favor a particular individual, but no one would count on this alone for economic success.

There is a strong respect for "science" in K'un Shen, which is undoubtedly the result of recent culture change as far as content is concerned, but the ease with which "science" has been accepted suggests an earlier pragmatism and openness to new methods which prove workable. People speak often of looking into "new ways" of doing things as well as learning the customary ways of doing things. "Newness" in itself is neither good nor bad. This fits in with the emphasis on human intelligence. K'un Shen is not fatalistic, in the usual sense that the world is used. Learning and using new techniques when old ones fail to work is acceptable. Where human intelligence fails, there is then recourse to the supernatural, or simply an attitude of forebearance. Some things are beyond control.

At this point one may ask why, if the society is receptive to new ideas, has there not been more change in the economic sphere? Actually, K'un Shen's traditionalism is misleading to some extent. While it is certainly true that sea fishing has changed little, except for the introduction of nylon nets, one cannot explain it adequately in terms of traditional values, reverence for the past, conservatism, or the like. The answer lies in the external realities, not in men's minds. There are no harbor facilities. There is no likelihood of securing the funds to build a harbor. There are no adequate loan facilities for modern equipment. The average fisherman is K'un Shen is well aware that if he had a motorboat and modern equipment, he would be able to increase his income, and he would be happy to do so, but there is no way for him to manage it. Similarly, techniques of pond cultivation have changed little over the past few generations, not because the villagers have rejected innovations, but because the technology has already reached the limits of improvement.

Some changes in material culture have been accepted in K'un Shen, as they have been in other Taiwanese communities. Dress, in particular, reflects foreign influences. Some new foods and methods of preparation have been accepted. House furnishings and sanitation have changed markedly in the past 50 years. A number of new items have come into the culture, first, as prestige items, later, to be taken for granted as a normal part of life: radios, pens, bicycles, plastic dishes, wristwatches, phonographs, sewing machines, cigarette lighters. The introduction of the radio has changed the musical style, and popular songs of American or Japanese origin have all but driven out the traditional folk music at the same time that it has spread a wider knowledge of Taiwanese opera. The acceptance of new items of material culture has led to a demand for a greater cash income, and in turn to an acceptance of new occupations.

Some members of the village, particularly the young, have shifted their jobs without any loss of prestige, and often with a gain in prestige. A variety of factory and shop jobs are now possible alternatives to sea fishing or pond cultivation. Practitioners of modern medicine enjoy very high prestige in the community, with new content added to a role that already had high prestige. To meet new demands, village merchants have added to their stock of goods, and peddlers and vendors sometimes specialize in goods that were unknown a generation ago.

Despite the rising standard of living in Taiwan and the development of new job opportunities, there is disagreement as to whether K'un Shen is benefiting or will benefit from these changes. The future seems uncertain, and few people are optimistic that their children's lives well be markedly better than were their own. However, most families are not completely satisfied with things as they are. That is, families in poor circumstances reject the idea that one necessarily has to be poor just because one's parents were poor. Poverty is not usually explained in terms of "fate," though there are other cultures where this is reported to be the case. Most people work hard and look for all possible means of income in an effort to keep the household going and raise it above its present level. They hope for change and improvement. However, they cannot commit themselves to saying that things will improve markedly; at most they say that things *could* improve, given education and effort. The Chinese reverence for the past does not extend to a reverence for poverty and hardship known in the past, and in this respect the people of the village are open and amenable to change.

3

Growing up in K'un Shen

Birth, Infancy, and Childhood

BIRTHS TAKE PLACE at home, usually, with the assistance of a midwife. Very few of the village women can afford to go to a city hospital, nor is it considered a necessity. Midwives usually are not consulted until the sixth or seventh month of pregnancy, to make sure that the baby is in the right position for birth. There are few changes in diet during pregnancy; the prospective mother may be advised to eat fruits and to supplement her diet with vitamins, but other foodstuffs are not specifically recommended.

If the pregnancy is a woman's first, her mother is sent for as soon as labor starts. Her mother-in-law, married sisters-in-law, and some neighboring women are also present. They *paipai*[1] with incense to help the delivery and bring water to wash the mother during and after labor. The husband is expected to be present to support the woman during labor. Labor is done in a kneeling position on the ground, or seated on a low stool. Formerly, grass and rice husks were spread on the floor, but now newspapers are used. If the birth is a difficult one, the midwife massages the mother's abdomen to "turn the child around." Drugs may be given to ease the pain, or an injection of an abortive drug administered. When the child emerges, the midwife cuts the umbilical cord with scissors. The cord and the afterbirth are buried afterward.

Three days after the birth the midwife visits the new mother, bathes the infant, and collects her fee. Delivery fees are not fixed. If the family is very poor, the midwife may collect only a token or nothing at all. If the family has an average income, the fee is between $60 and $80 NT. Twins are a disappointment to the family, and regarded as a misfortune, so in twin births the midwife receives only $30 NT. The midwife is held responsible for the welfare of the child during its first month of life, but if it dies after that time, she is not blamed.

---

[1] The term *paipai* can be used generally to mean a festival or worship or, more specifically, as here, to mean praying, bowing, kneeling, and offering incense to the gods.

The new mother is given boiled eggs and cake immediately after the birth to help her regain her strength. Her own mother brings special strengthening foods for her, such as chicken, pork, liver, noodles, ginger, and bananas. (Duck is to be avoided at the birth of the first child, lest the baby grow up ugly as a duck). These foods are often cooked together with strengthening herbs. The new mother must eat plenty of meat, but in poor families this is hard to provide. Ideally, she remains in the house resting for a full month after birth.

Twelve days after birth, the infant is given its first haircut, and another bath. In the water are placed two eggs and a stone, to make the baby's face as "pretty as an eggshell" and his head "hard as stone," which means, in this context, wise. Also on the twelfth day after birth the new mother prepares a special dish of fried rice with meat and shrimp and presents these to the neighboring women, who in turn bring uncooked rice and red paper to congratulate her.

At the end of the first month, the maternal grandmother visits again, bringing with her clothing for the baby, a carrying cloth, a blanket, and red cakes. The young mother's household prepares both sweet and salty fried rice for her to take back home. If the child is a first child, the maternal grandmother must bring either 6 or 12 dishes of different foods. The end of the first month is marked by offerings of thanks to the Bed-mother goddess (*Chng-bu*) for preserving the new mother and infant. The mother's isolation is new ended. She is again free to participate in social events such as weddings and temple festivals. She may go outside without a head-covering and at any time (confinement during the first month is not absolute and most women do leave their rooms after the first 12 days), whereas before she could not emerge after the stars appeared.

Almost all infants are breast fed. If the mother's milk is scanty, there are sometimes supplemental feedings of tinned milk or powdered milk available from the village general stores. More often, however, there is recourse to a wet nurse, a nursing relative, or feedings of rice water. Infants are fed on demand or when the mother has free time. There is no keeping to a schedule for feedings. In fact, the idea of a schedule is abhorrent; younger mothers in the village have heard of such practices, but reject them.

After the sixth or seventh month, infants begin to receive some solid foods in small amounts, while breast feeding continues. The child is fed soft rice, mashed pieces of cake or cookies, a small piece of meat to suck on, or mashed fish. The earliest time for weaning is when the baby has completed 12 full months of life, and most children are weaned within the following year. However, there are a few children who are not weaned until three years or more in age, and about one-third of the children are weaned between the ages of two and three. This late weaning occurs when the mother feels that the child is in poor health.

When weaning comes, it is sudden. The mother paints her nipple with bitter herbs, red pepper, ginger, or garlic, or smears it with lipstick so that it appears to bleed, or tells the child that is is filled with excrement. When the child cries for food, he is given cake or rice, and if he continues to cry, he is held by the mother or carried on her back until he falls asleep.

Babies usually sleep next to the mother on the *tatami* mats or hard platforms. During the day, they are either put to sleep there or carried in a cloth sling on their mother's back while she works or walks, or they are placed in a swinging cradle for several hours each day. When the baby is four or five months' old, it can be placed in a bamboo chair with a bar across to keep it from falling out. Children are carried on backs as soon as they have some control over their neck muscles and can hold their heads up. They usually are not carried this way after they are two-and-one-half or three years of age.

Carrying the child on her back, the mother soon becomes sensitized to motions or cries indicating that the child is about to urinate or defecate and she removes it from her back and holds it over the ground or a ditch to relieve itself. Toilet training thus begins at a very early age, for when the child urinates the mother makes a whistling sound. Soon, she begins holding the child and making the whistling sound to encourage it to urinate. However, serious toilet training does not begin until the end of the first year. Most children are toilet trained by the time they are two. Rapid toilet training is facilitated by the wearing of split pants; all the child has to do is squat in order not to soil its clothing. As soon as it can understand, it is encouraged to squat over the nearest ditch or on the dirt floor. Use of the outhouse is not encouraged until the age of four or five.

When an infant is one-month old, his name is registered in the household records kept at the police station. What is given is his family name and a two-character formal name. This is not the name by which he is called or spoken of during infancy and early childhood, or even into the teens. In address, in later years, the formal name is often suffixed with "ah" to make it less formal, and during infancy the name for reference and address usually incorporates one character of the formal name, and is both suffixed and prefexed by "ah." Thus, a girl whose formal name is *Yu-hsiang* (jade fragrance) is called *"Hsiang'ah"* or *"Ah-hsiang"* as an infant and young child, and when she becomes a teenager, it is lengthened to *"Yu-hsiang-ah."* Often, the child acquires a nickname in addition to these names, and it may stick through childhood; one unfortunate five-year-old was always called "Big-nose," in complete disregard of his formal name or baby names.

Names are subject to change. If the infant is frequently ill, it is usually thought a good practice to change his formal name and his baby name, thus confusing whatever spirits might be making him ill. These changes do not always appear in the household records, so that the legal name under which the child is eventually registered at school may be a discarded name used not at all by one's relatives and friends. Names are also changed if it is discovered that some other relative has the same name.

Brothers usually share the first character of their given name in common, and the same is sometimes done with sisters. Names for boys favor such words as "mountain," "water," "wood," "field," and, occasionally, "virtue," "peace," or "prosperity." Girls names tend toward "fragrant," "beautiful," "spring," "autumn," "gold," and are more likely to be comprised on only one character prefaced by "ah," even for the formal name, then are boys names.

The 3-year-old is already fairly self-reliant. He can feed himself, albeit awkwardly. From this age on children eat apart from the adults until they reach the age of 10 or 11. They are given their bowl of rice or sweet potato topped with a few bits of meat and vegetable and sent outside to join the other children. During the day they are given snacks of cake, cookies, candies, or fruits.

The child is toilet trained and weaned by the age of three. He is allowed out of the house by himself, where he can play alone or with other toddlers, usually under the watchful eye of an older sibling. He is also at the age where he can be punished for his mistakes, though not severely because he is too young to have understanding of what he has done wrong. He is still very dependent physically on his mother. Children do not begin dressing themselves until four or five years of age, and are not thought capable of bathing themselves until six or seven. By the time the youngster reaches the age when he can begin fending for himself his mother is already involved with a new baby. Perhaps because of this there is a tendency to violent tantrums among the preschool toddlers. They are easily driven to total rage, and lie kicking and screaming on the ground, ignored by the adults.

Tantrums are not punishable any more than lapses in toilet training, and they are regarded as something that will pass in time. The three-year-old, however, does face punishments for disobedience to parental requests or rules, or physical attacks on a younger sibling or a neighbor's child. Beating with a twig or stick is the most common form of punishment, and the blows are usually directed at the child's legs. Hitting a child's head or face is a serious punishment, and rarely employed. Verbal scolding and cursings are also common. Another form of punishment is to threaten the child with the possibility that he will be given away for adoption to some far off family. My presence in the community inspired a variant: I would take the child to America, a horrendous punishment, judging from the reactions it could evoke. There are other threats which will frighten a child into contrition and obedience; a number of mothers threaten that the policeman or soldiers will take the child away, or say that a cat or dog is coming. However, they do not invoke the threat of ghosts, for this is *too* frightening, even for adults. Food deprivation is also used as a punishment, but more often it is an empty threat, with the parent relenting and giving the child its meal anyway. Some mothers use the same pattern followed with tantrums, completely ignoring the child, pretending not to hear anything it says, and of course not speaking to it or about it. Or the child may see his siblings get some special treat, which he is not allowed to share. Another form of punishment, resorted to only for very serious matters, is to tie the child up, hanging from its wrists, often accompanied by a beating.

Fighting with other children is one of the most serious offenses a child can commit. At best they get a scolding from their parents. Often they are beaten, regardless of who started the fight, though the child who was not the initial aggressor is more likely to receive only a verbal reprimand. Children soon learn that the most effective action when someone hits them is to to report it to the aggressor's mother, who will herself punish her child. However, one mother confessed that she only pretended to hit her own child when a neighbor or neighbor's child complained that her own had started a fight.

Hitting or teasing younger siblings is also strongly frowned on. Some mothers will beat the older child whatever the circumstances of the quarrel. Most lecture and scold the older child, pointing out that siblings should love one another and get along well together. The younger is almost always less blamed, since he has lesser understanding of how to behave.

The noisy, whining, or crying child is sometimes slapped or scolded, but the more usual course of action is to coax and bribe the child into more social behavior. Thus, the youngster soon learns that a constant whining will net him a few pennies and an admonition to "go outside and play." In infancy, the breast is used as a pacifier, even when the child has just recently finished eating, and in a continuation of the pattern, the older child is given a piece of cake or cookies, or some money for candy, in order to quiet him. Otherwise, the adults may try to ignore and talk above the racket the child is creating, until eventually their nerves are worn down and they respond with a slap or a bribe for quiet. If the child is still fairly small, the mother may hold him or carry him on her back for a while, particularly if he has been but recently weaned.

Punishments are also administered to children who hurt themselves while playing, the punishment coming before the cut or bruise is attended to. The child's body is not thought of as his exclusive property; it is a gift from the parents and should be handled carefully to avoid injury. The child who is careless and wounds himself has failed his parents and deserves at least a slap, if not a beating, as well as a lengthy scolding. The child soon learns to be cautious in his playing. The games played by older children are mild ones which do not hold any danger of injury. The swings, climbing bars, and seesaws installed in the school playground get relatively little use. Tree climbing may be a temptation, but is is permitted only under watchful parental eyes when fruit has to be picked. The beach and fish ponds are off limits to children. They are not encouraged to learn to swim and few do.

Respect for one's body mingles with puritanism in the attitude toward masturbation. Some parents deny that their children do this at all. If a child is discovered masturbating he is severely scolded and beaten. He is threatened with what will happen if he continues; he will be unable to urinate, or he will go crazy. Children are also expected to conceal their genitalia from the eyes of others. If a boy urinates outside, he must use his hand to conceal his genitals, while girls past the age of four are expected to use the privacy of the *benjo* where no one can see them. They are reprimanded with slaps and scoldings if they expose themselves.

Children are provided with very few toys, and most of these are homemade. Kite flying is one of the popular amusements for boys between the ages of 7 and 12, and sometimes teenagers or even adult men will indulge. Only rarely is the kite a purchased and elaborate one; more often it is made at home from newspaper and bamboo. This seems to be mainly a winter sport. Some boys own tops. Girls of the same ages jump rope or play "potsy." Children of both sexes play chess. Baseball, a recent import, is played mostly by boys' with improvised bats, but the outfield is occasionally filled out with girls. Another "game" is to make an earth oven and roast sweet potatoes. After festivals, the boys sometimes outline a circle with stones and pretend to "fire walk" with the god's chair. Girls play at imitating laundering or cooking, and both sexes play "school" until the age where these games become realities. I do not recall ever seeing girls playing with dolls, though they are manufactured in Taiwan. Care of younger siblings begins around the age of five for both sexes, obviating the need for dolls.

At Moon Festival, the fifteenth of the eighth lunar month, there is a special game for children. The group stands in a circle, with one in the center who is "it." The children repeatedly chant a song:

> Frog-spirit, Frog, hop!
> The fifteenth of the eighth moon,
> Come here and hop!

After some five minutes of increasing intensity, the children waving sticks of incense in the air as they sing, the child who is "it" becomes possessed and imitates the movements of a frog, causing great laughter not only among the children but also among the watching adults. The child who was "it" usually leaves the game after he recovers, but the game goes on until the others tire. The game is very popular with both boys and girls between the ages of about 4 and 12.

Adults rarely play with children or joke with them, fearing that their discipline over the child will be weakened if they do so. Similarly, few adults will have conversations with children since children are not capable of understanding much and because, again, it may weaken parental authority. Aside from lullabies for babies the mothers do not sing to the children, nor do other adult household members teach them songs or rhymes. If there is an older sibling attending school, the child learns some songs and rhymes from him. Similarly, few parents tell the children stories: It is the older siblings who bring back tales heard in class or read in books and tell them to the younger children, or a grandparent with leisure time who amuses the children with a story. Conversations between parents and children are minimal. When parents talk to children, they have instructions to give them, or requests to make, or feel compelled to lecture or scold them. Thus, it is not surprising that the children turn to each other, or to a grandparent, to talk about the things that have happened to them during the day, and about their desires and interests. Mothers are less remote from the children than are fathers—their punishments tend to be less severe and they are more likely to give the child sweets or a few pennies for candy. Many children find their fathers frightening and unapproachable. A father's words have more authority than a mother's, since the mother is prone to idle threats and vague statements about what will happen "next time," or fails to follow through on punishments, as when she weakens and brings the child supper after all, or gives him a perfunctory tap for fighting with another child. The more serious breaches are left to the father for punishment, with the result that heavy beatings or other forms of physical punishment are more often associated with the father than with the mother. If father offers a reprimand, the child is likely to take it more seriously. That father is also empowered to beat mother makes him even more terrifying in the child's eyes and allies him with his mother, despite the fact that she also is a punishing agent.

The early years of childhood are still pleasant ones for most children. They are free to roam the village, taking in the sights and finding excitement where they can. Puppet shows and operas occur often enough to break the monotony, and any new arrival in the village such as a medicine seller or picturebook salesman instantly draws a crowd of children. The children cluster around at any ceremonial event, including weddings, and funerals of households unrelated to theirs. They play everywhere and anywhere in the village, and are rarely chased away. There are hundreds of other children to play with and even one's immediate neighborhood is guaranteed to have several children of the same age, give or take a year.

Work responsibilities begin around age 6. Children are asked to perform a variety of chores: gathering wood for the fire, tending the fire and cooking pot, sweeping the courtyard, carrying the baby outside, running errands to the stores or stalls for the adults in the household. As they grow older, around 11 or 12, they are able to take on jobs that bring in a small income, such as shucking oysters or helping to haul fishing nets. The sooner a child can begin earning money the better, and the children are constantly reminded of the importance of being a wage earner.

During childhood, there is relatively little indulgence in the way of material goods. Most families are far too poor to be able to buy new clothing, and so the same garments are handed down to one sibling after another, mended and patched until they fall apart. The best foods at the table go to the adults, not the children. Only rarely does a child get a choice morsel from the table, or a new outfit to wear.

The Village School and Formal Education

The village school serves the children of K'un Shen as well as some of the children from the nearest fishing village, and has been in existence in one form or another since the turn of the century. Just prior to the beginning of Japanese rule, a private school was established in the village for the purpose of teaching the Chinese classics and preparing boys for taking the official examinations. It was held in the village temple and had a small attendance. With the start of Japanese rule, the temple school was transformed into a modern primary school, at times under a Japanese headmaster, and for a time under a Taiwanese headmaster. From a temple side room it moved into straw huts and then in 1921 into more permanent wooden buildings at the site where the school now stands.

The school provides the basic six-year primary-school education that is prescribed by the provincial government, using standard texts and class programs. The first two grades meet for three hours of classes every day except Sunday. Of these, seven hours a week are spent learning to read and write. Since none of the village children are native speakers of Mandarin, these seven hours are also language instruction. All classroom conversations and instruction are supposed to be carried out in Mandarin. Another two hours during the week are devoted to "Common Knowledge," introductory general materials on Chinese history, geography, civics, and natural science. An additional half-hour is used for a class meeting. The rest of the school time in the first two grades is used for singing and music instruction and drawing and handicrafts such as cutting and pasting paper. This latter part of the curriculum causes great puzzlement to the parents, who do not regard this as a necessary part of the children's education.

In the first two grades, the child attends only half-day. In the third and fourth grades, instruction time is extended another half-hour each day so that the children attend both in the morning and in the afternoon. Arithmetic and use of the abacus are added to the curriculum (a total of three-and-one-half hours per week), and the amount of time spent on drawing, handicrafts, and music is cut to provide an hour and a half of composition, and an additional half-hour of Common Knowledge instruction.

In the fifth and sixth grades, the school day is extended to four-and-a-half hours daily. History, geography, and natural science are taught as separate subjects, two hours of the latter and one hour each of the former each week. Writing of characters becomes a separate subject, with an hour and a half devoted each week to improving the students' writing. A final addition to the curriculum is one which has met with some opposition from both parents and students: two-and-a-half hours each week of physical education.

The teaching staff are mainly Taiwanese, and mostly women. Only a few are from the village or resident there. They are also quite young in terms of the expectations the villagers have about the proper age for a teacher; that is, they are in their early twenties. As a result, the villagers do not have complete confidence that they are able to discipline the children and teach them proper moral behavior.

Parents question the ability of the teachers. They also object to such frills as physical education, painting, handicrafts, and music. The general feeling is that the school need only teach the children to read and write, to speak Mandarin, and to learn some arithmetic. Often, the goal of education is summed up as learning to "recognize characters." Its practical advantage is that a person will be able to travel without getting lost, and can send letters to the family when away from home. Mandarin is counted necessary for boys, since they will eventually be drafted into the army and have to take orders in Mandarin: If they do not understand, they will find army life too difficult. For girls, the ability to speak Mandarin is not regarded as essential. Arithmetic also has its value, for a person who can handle numbers will not be so easily cheated in business dealings.

The village school is tuition free, but the students must purchase their own supplies and textbooks. Though this is not a major expense, many parents feel it to be an unnecessary burden, and there is little enthusiasm for any other extra expenses the school may involve, such as outings and field trips.

Informal interviews with each of the members of the school staff indicated that they all felt a lack of enthusiasm and support for the school on the part of the parents. Some were concerned with the low motivation of their students. The truancy rate has been declining, but on days when there is net hauling a high percentage of pupils in the upper grades do not come to class or fail to complete their homework for the next day. Teachers who have taught previously in city schools find that the village children are less responsive and less interested, except for the few who come from the wealthier village homes.

The pupils' level of classroom performance is disappointing to some of the teachers, whose previous contacts have been with children in the city. Many of their disappointments are the same as those facing their American counterparts who do their student teaching with children of the middle class (and children of the faculty), and then are sent into a slum neighborhood or small rural school. One hears complaints that the children fall asleep in class or seem inattentive. Often the children have not gone to sleep until 11:00 or 12:00 P.M., and have been up since dawn. Some have not eaten before coming to school. Many have health problems which interfere with their efficiency in class. The school's estimate of the incidence of tra-choma, for example, was 43 percent of the pupils.

There are other reasons beyond the obvious ones of crowded living, poor nutrition, and health. The children of K'un Shen are not prepared to compete and to achieve in the school situation. Their home training has not encouraged them to display their cleverness or volunteer answers and information. On the contrary, they have been trained to keep silence in the presence of adults, and most of what they say at home is ignored. Moreover, the majority come from families where the parents cannot teach them to read and write prior to entry into school, and from families where the parents have little time to spend with the children or see little reason for doing so.

In addition, children receive relatively little praise for their accomplishments. Most parents feel it is not good for the child to be praised lest he become complacent. A child may be scolded or beaten for failing to do well because the parents feel that he is not utilizing his full potential, but the child who *does* do well usually receives no praise as his reward. The feeling is that he has done as he should, and perhaps he could do even better; if praised, he will not expend effort to do better. The result is that the children are often unsure of themselves, lacking in self-confidence and hesitant to take an active part in their classwork. The grading system contributes to this. The child does not know how well he has done in relation to the amount of work he is supposed to have mastered; he knows only how well he has done as compared to others in his class. If he stands in the top ten, he feels a surge of confidence. If he stands in the bottom ten, he may lapse into indifference, and his parents will take this as a proof that he was not meant to go to school.

Finally, there is the growing feeling of obligation and guilt that one finds as the children move into the upper grades, the feeling that their education is a privilege and luxury to which they are not really entitled. They talk of having to "repay" their parents for allowing them to go to school this long, and speak of "going out into society" to earn money to pay back their debts. Prevalent in the community is the idea that education is a luxury or privilege to which the poor are not entitled. This, despite the fact that the tuition is free and the expenses low, is sufficient to quell parental enthusiasm for the school. If parents do let the child complete all six years, it is for reasons aside from the "value" of education in and of itself. There is the recognition that the girls will make more advantagious marriages if they have completed primary school or are at least literate. There is also the realization that they will be able to take a factory job for a few years before they marry and help to defray the dowry costs in that way. For the boys, the problems illiterates encounter in the army are often the reason given for allowing sons to complete a primary-school education, but parents are ambivalent about giving the boys enough education so that they can find work outside of the village, for reasons given earlier.

Generally, the idea of mass education has not been accepted. Most of the people in the parental generation and nearly all in the grandparental generations are illiterate, and there has been no attempt at erasing adult illiteracy. In the eyes of the village adults, if the student is just average or mediocre, he does not belong in school, not even in the first six years of primary school. Having had no experience with formal education themselves, they find it difficult to assess the amount of learning that the child has done from the grades he receives. If his grades are toward the middle or bottom of the class, it is a sign to them that he is not fitted for school. Again, if the child seems disinterested in his schoolwork, there is little attempt to encourage or force the child to study, and of course few parents can actually give help. There is the feeling that the disinterested child does not "deserve" to be a student and therefore should leave school.

For those who complete the village primary school, there is theoretically the chance of continuing on to junior middle school and perhaps even to senior middle school and the university, but relatively few children from K'un Shen advance beyond the village school. The reasons are again varied. One problem is that of adequate preparation. In actuality, the time spent in the classrooms does not provide the children with the necessary skills and knowledge needed to pass the entrance examinations into the junior middle schools. In K'un Shen, as elsewhere in Taiwan, these are gained largely through private classes held after regular school hours by the school staff. Of the class that graduated in 1962, some 25 students out of 83 attended these private classes, at a cost of $30 NT per month. Not surprisingly, they came from the wealthier families in the village, and in some cases from the better-educated families. A few of the parents from the latter group attended the sessions from time to time in order to be able to give the children further coaching at home.

Even if the family has the money and motivation to register the children in these private classes, there is no guarantee that they will gain admission to the middle schools. The examinations are fiercely competitive, and they will of course be competing with children from the city school system who have access to better schools, a choice of private tutors, and home backgrounds often superior in education and sophistication to those in K'un Shen.

In addition, there is the factor of economic pressures beyond the costs of private tutoring classes, for the middle-school students must commute daily to the city, which means bus fares or a bicycle and provision for lunch. They need more expensive school uniforms and equipment fees, and of course the family will be deprived of the potential income of the student and of help in daily chores or jobs around the village. One cannot ask a middle-school student to help with net hauling when he comes back to the village in the early evening, or expect him to neglect his homework in order to look after younger siblings.

Finally, although most of the fishermen's families will concede that the children should have some training in the primary school, education beyond that point is seen as a great luxury, a privilege for the rich, and an undertaking only for the very brightest and ablest students. It is far beyond the dreams of most.

The Green Years

It is difficult to draw the dividing line between childhood and adulthood. The term *gina* can apply to anyone between infancy and the age of 30, and while the term is usually translated to mean "child," its underlying meaning seems to be that the individual in question has not reached an age of social maturity or responsibility. Students at all ages, including university students, are *gina* and so are unemployed youths who engage in the Taiwan equivalent of juvenile-delinquent behavior, or young people who are known to go to movies, visit the red-light districts, or engage in similar kinds of activity. After a person has a permanent job and has married (events which occur around the same time, in one's early twenties) people outside the household cease using the term *gina,* but it may continue to be used within the household, even after he has become the functioning household head with children of his own, if his parents are still present.

Yet there is something of a transitional stage between childhood and adulthood, the years between the end of primary school and the beginnings of married life, even though there is no distinct "teen-age culture." In some households the sixteenth year is taken as the mark-off point after which one begins to be an adult. On the seventh day of the seventh month a *paipai* is made to the Goddess of the Great Dipper *Chit-seng-hu-zin* to signify that the child is now grown up and ready to leave the family or take on adult responsibility. The youngster in whose honor the ceremony is performed receives new clothing and, if a girl, ornaments and cosmetics. These gifts come from parents, and also from father's sisters' and mother's brothers' households. The celebrating household distributes red cakes to the neighbors and friends and holds a feast for them. They in turn make a money contribution to the feast. The friends of the young person are not invited. However, even with formal *rite de passage,* the boy or girl continues to be a *gina* for several more years at least.

The onset of puberty, several years earlier, tends to be ignored. Menstruation is a taboo topic, and most girls are not forewarned about its occurrence. Thus, the onset of menses causes considerable fear and anxiety. If the girl has an older sister or sympathetic young sister-in-law, she confides in her and then receives some information. Otherwise, several months may pass before the girl finds the courage to tell her mother what is happening, and many mothers have no idea of when the daughter first began to menstruate. The menstrual flow is generally regarded as shameful, dirty, and ritually defiling.

Nor do parents feel it necessary to provide information about sexual matters. Despite the fact that the child continues to share the parental bedroom, and the parental bed, until well into primary school, people are convinced that the children are completely unaware of sexual intercourse. Indeed, there does seem to be some kind of block that operates. Many women say that until their marriage they had no idea at all that intercourse took place between married couples, and the men claim outside sources for their information. Most have their first sexual experiences in their late teens, when an older boy takes them into the city to visit the prostitution district.

The girls are more sheltered. Even when a girl is about to be married, there is no attempt to instruct her on sexual matters. Most women would feel embarrassed to discuss the subject with their daughters. The premarital advice that they give is limited to such things as proper behavior toward in-laws and obedience to one's husband. There is also folk advice. If you step on your husband's shoes before you get into bed on the wedding night, you will be able to have more control over your husband, or if you remember to sleep next to the wall, you will live to a ripe old age. None of it relates to sex.

Today, some information about sex is transmitted via the mass media. There are simple sex manuals that circulate clandestinely among young adults, and there are the occasional Japanese or American movies, which are somewhat more explicit about heterosexual relationships than are the Chinese films. The young people are no longer quite as innocent as their parents would like to believe.

Information about birth is also a taboo subject from childhood through the teen years. When a baby is being born, the children are shooed away from the room or even from the house. They are told later that the mother "found" the baby somewhere, or brought it from somebody's home, or that it came out of a stone that was split open. Some parents will say that the mother gave birth to it, without any further explanation, and the child who persists in questioning will be scolded and told not to ask more questions. However, children are usually allowed to watch animals giving birth, or animals having intercourse. The feeling is that they will not understand what is happening anyway, and no adult would offer an explanation to them.

Training in modesty begins at an early age, and from the age of about 12 on the girls must show even more decorum than before. They must sit straight with their legs together, and when sleeping, they must lie on their side, with legs pressed together. If the girl's mother sees her sitting or sleeping in another position she will strike her on the legs or scold her severely. Girls at this age are supposed to try to speak softly, and to cover their mouths when they laugh. They are also expected to dress modestly.

There is little open social contact between teen-aged boys and girls. Children in K'un Shen play together in mixed groups until about nine years of age. After that, they separate by sex, under pressure from teasing by parents and elder siblings. The school reinforces this by seating the sexes separately and discouraging coeducational play during recess. In more traditional times, this segregation would continue through adolescence, but there are indications that even then it was not strictly enforced. In the evenings it is customary for the young people to dress in their better clothes and walk around the village, the girls and boys moving in separate groups. From within the security of the group they will exchange a few remarks with someone of the opposite sex. There is no visible "pairing off." The newly organized 4-H Club in the community provides some opportunities for social mingling, though usually the boys and girls meet in different sections. Class-reunion parties, held in the evening at the school, offer another newly created situation where adolescent boys and girls can meet without parental supervision. These parties are held once a year, with about 80% attendance. The members contribute money to buy cakes and soft drinks, and sit around chatting while they eat. Again, girls sit separately from boys, but it is a coeducational affair nonetheless.

Young people who work in the city during the day have something of an advantage; boys and girls find excuses to travel there together or to meet in the city.

Somehow, despite the restrictions, love affairs do develop among the young people, and some of them result in marriages. Only after the couple become formally engaged will the community sanction an approximation of "dating." However, since there is no well-defined dating pattern in Taiwanese culture, it is more than likely that a boy and girl left alone together will engage in sexual relations. This is feared by the older people. If a boy and girl are discovered to have met secretly somewhere, it is assumed that they had sexual intercourse, or were planning to. The girl's reputation is seriously threatened, and if the couple want to marry, the parents are usually quick to acquiesce.

The teen years are still childhood years. Many teen-agers are neither in school nor employed. They take odd jobs around the village, and help with the household chores. They are allowed to join the adults at the dining table, but they do not take part in family decision making and they enter only occasionally into the general conversation. If they are employed, most of their earnings are turned back to the family. They are still firmly under parental authority.

Adult Roles and the Good Person

With marriage and steady employment, the individual gradually takes on more and more power to make decisions and control his own daily activities. From *gina* he eventually moves to the position of household head, functioning with some autonomy from parents and from elders in closely related households.

Income and wealth are only a part of the basis for judging a person's social standing. Public opinion defines what characteristics an adult should have in order to be respected and esteemed in the community. Moderation is the keynote in behavior. With children and teen-agers, a lack of moderation is criticized and punished. For adults, censure is even stronger, and village gossip bears down on those who stray too far from the norms of behavior.

Drinking, for example, is strongly condemned, and is very rarely seen in the village. Its absence is not to be taken as an indicator of poverty, for there are poorer peasant communities elsewhere in the world where heavy drinking *is* the norm. Here, intoxication is not sought, although alcoholic beverages are available for ceremonial occasions. Drinking is frowned on and feared because it is accompanied by a lack of control, and with that letdown of discipline a man may do things that will shame him in the eyes of his neighbors and relatives. Heavy drinking by men is reserved for those rare occasions when they go to the city to visit prostitutes, and women seldom taste liquor, even at family feasts.

Fighting, quarreling, and show of temper are also severely frowned on because they indicate a lack of control. Childhood training stresses the importance of suppressing aggressive impulses, and by adulthood feelings are supposed to be under control. The man who is angered will, if he meets the ideal, become even more soft-spoken and smile more frequently as he talks. In daily life, the incidence of physical violence between peers is very rare. Men do not get involved in fist fights or wrestling bouts with one another, nor do women. Some quarrels occur at the verbal level, even though verbal aggression is not sanctioned. People shout and curse at one another when strongly angered. There is also some physical release of aggression permitted via physical assault on a subordinate. The beating of children by parents or of the wife by her husband seems sometimes to go far beyond the immediate cause for the punishment, and becomes an opportunity for the superior to rid himself of much repressed rage.

The person who is courteous and in control of his emotions is highly regarded in the community. Formal politeness is not elaborate, as among the Taiwanese upper classes. Most people in the village are not educated enough to include polite literary phrases in their conversation. There is, however, a working level of courtesy that includes greetings, an amount of warmth that is expressed toward others regardless of their economic position, the stock show of interest in another's activities and welfare that keep persons on a friendly basis even if they are not emotionally close.

Indeed, intense emotionality of any sort is discouraged. The mature person does not openly express rage or hatred, nor does he usually express strong feelings of pleasure or love. He strives to maintain an even emotional level, and when, being human, he momentarily loses control, he exposes himself to gossip and ridicule. Funerals are one of the few times when a person is permitted to show strong emotion, and even in this situation, the emotions are controlled; there are times during the funeral ceremony when one wails and cries and other times when one keeps quiet. The opera performances at festivals provide another occasion when tears are permitted, and the "soap operas" on the afternoon radio broadcasts are also an excuse for emotionality. In daily life, however, one "plays it cool," to borrow an American term, or one tries to "keep one's cool," giving no visible sign of extreme emotions of any kind. There is rehearsal for this through childhood. Children cry very little after the age of four or thereabouts, even when they are hurt. Their faces reflect little of the curiosity they must feel when they cluster around to watch some unusual occurrence. Wild laughing, shouting, running, and other expressions of high spirits are discouraged.

There is little privacy for anyone. For most of one's time, waking or sleeping, one is in the company of others: kinsmen, neighbors, workmates. As we might expect, the community puts a high rating on the ability to cooperate and get along with others. The good person is reliable and industrious, willing to do his own part of the work and to extend help to others, and generous with time and money. Moreover, he is cautious and circumspect in his speech, keeping human relations smooth.

To say that a person "speaks carelessly" (o-peq-kong) is a serious criticism. The person who gossips too much or who misleads people with his words endangers the functioning of the group. When people talk about someone they strongly dislike, this accusation of "careless speech" is frequently made. In some contexts it means "liar," a warning that nothing this person says should be credited. In other contexts it means that the person is mistaken in what he says, but often with an undertone of meaning that the person should not be so quick to spread false information. In still other contexts, it means only that the person talks too much; the truth or falsity of what he says is not the issue. Gossip is one of the main forms of recreation and tension release in the village, but a person has to know where to draw the line and be quiet.

Self-aggrandizement is frequently criticized, whether it takes the form of boasting about one's own accomplishments, or ridiculing and belittling the activities of others. The control of the former is provided for in childhood training, where children get little praise from their parents for any accomplishments. As an adult, the individual is quiet about what he has done, and if another person lauds him, he is embarrassed and self-effacing.

Perhaps the most crucial positive trait that the adult individual must show is the willingness to work hard and make maximal use of work time. The word for recreation is the same word used for the play of young children (*chit-thou*), and it has negative connotations when applied to adults or near adults. The teen-age person or young adult who seeks recreation is called a "playing child" (*chit-thou-gina*). Even on the first days of the New Year holiday, most of the villagers work, in contrast to city people and peasants in farming communities who take at least a day or two of rest in celebration. On the days of temple festivals, most of the men go out to work as usual in the mornings, and attend the festival only after they have put in long working hours. Recreation certainly has its place, but it cannot be overdone. Spare time is, in a sense, nonexistent.

Because of the emphasis on work, there is a falling off of prestige as the person moves into old age. K'un Shen gives lip service to the Confucian ideas of respect for age, but in actuality there are few people of advanced years who can attract respect and maintain authority, unless they belong to the small group of educated property owners. They then continue to have a voice as village leaders and mediators. Fishermen, however, retire from their economic roles around the age of fifty, relinquishing active headship of the household around the same time. There is little that men can do after reaching old age. Around the village, one sees them helping the women bind brushwood, or looking after one of their grandchildren, or just sitting silently in the sun, waiting. The elderly women fare slightly better, for household chores are not as demanding physically and they continue performing them well into old age. Dependent on the younger generations for support, they

A game of chess helps pass the time for aging men.

gradually subordinate themselves to the wishes of their juniors and resign themselves to death.

Death and Funeral Procedures

The time of death is believed by many to be predetermined. Death, therefore, is met with acceptance and resignation, particularly if the dying person is of advanced age. The onset of illness or sudden debilitation in an elderly person is often taken as the sign of approaching death, so that the family will begin funeral preparations well before death occurs. In many families, advance arrangements are made to purchase a coffin. Even so, the coffin is usually not stored in the home and arrives only when the person is considered close to death. These and other preparations signify that death is close at hand.

For example, there was a women in her eighties who had been in poor health for several years and during the winter suddenly became seriously ill with pneumonia and other complications. Some six days before she died, she was moved into the central room of the house. There, she was dressed by her daughter-in-law in the clothing she would wear at burial: a white underdress, black trousers, six black jackets, and cotton shoes. Her hair was combed for the occasion. A paper sedan chair and two paper figures of chair carriers were placed in the central room with her. However, in case the family had made an error in judgment, a doctor (Western trained) was called in to attend her and to confirm the family's expectation that she was near the end. When he did confirm this, the coffin was ordered.

The clothing prepared for the dead are known as *ta baq lieng,* and the number of layers worn by the person reflects the wealth of the family and importance of the deceased. A really wealthy man will have some 12 layers of clothing, an ordinary person around 5 or 6, while a poor person can expect only 3. The number of offerings made during the funeral services are in proportion to the *ta baq lieng,* particularly the number of wine libations made. For all, be they rich or poor, the white undergarment is standard and must be provided by the daughters of the deceased. The other items come from sons and grandsons.

The time between death and actual burial varies in relation to the wealth of the family. The poor are buried a day or so after their death. Households of ordinary income hold the funeral some 10 to 15 days after death, and some of the wealthier village households will wait 30 days. A very wealthy person might not be buried until 100 days have elapsed. The woman just mentioned, who came from one of the better-off households, was buried 10 days after death, although the family originally announced that it would hold the funeral some 45 days after her death. During the time between death and burial, the body is kept in the central room of the house, sealed in the large heavy coffin. Paper money, rough paper, and lime are also placed in the coffin.

Between the time of death and burial there are various restrictions on mourners. Sons, and the close friends of sons are not allowed to bathe, cut their hair, or shave; close friends of sons are included because the dead person has treated them like sons, particularly if they are sworn brothers. Mourners are restricted from visiting the village temple, carrying the god's chairs, or fire walking during religious ceremonies. Close mourners are also expected to wear coarse clothing, close mourners here referring to sons, daughters, daughters-in-law, spouse, grandchildren, siblings, male first cousins, and brother's children.

The burden of funeral costs are born by the household of the deceased and married-out daughters. Until recently, the village had burial societies which were cooperative ventures between neighbors and relatives. The number of members in a society was around 40; if a person had both parents still living, he "joined" twice so that the number of memberships was always more than the number of members. The societies assisted at a death by carrying the coffin, or donating a sum of money to hire a coffin carrier. They lent tables and dishes for the funeral feast, and gave assistance in the work tasks associated with the funeral such as setting up tents. This cut the costs somewhat, but the main burden still fell on the family. At present, people depend on friends and neighbors for these services on an informal reciprocal basis, with a token gift of $1 or $2 NT and invitation to the funeral feast as payment: If someone is approached and asked to help, he is expected to comply, unless he has a pressing reason for not doing so. At the time of death friends and more distant relatives send a small sum of money, between $30 and $50 NT, to the household of the deceased. According to informants, it is only close friends who do this.

As soon as possible after the person dies, he is dressed in his burial clothes, if this has not already been done, and a paper sedan chair is burned to announce his death. Messages are dispatched to relatives around the village and elsewhere, and usually a Taoist priest is sent for that same day or the next morning to chant prayers for the dead. Married daughters living elsewhere come as soon as possible to weep for the dead. If the burial is to be delayed more than a few days, they will return to their husband's home for the interim. Seven days after death, it is customary to call in Taoist or Buddhist priests to hold the first of a series of masses known as *sun* which are repeated every 7 days for the next 6 weeks or at 10-day intervals. Another mass must be said 100 days after death. Many families cannot afford to observe the whole series and hold *sun* only once before the funeral and again once afterward. It is also important during this interim period that the house be prepared properly for the funeral. The red paper strips on the doorway are covered over with more appropriate inscriptions signify mourning, as, for example, "Our imploring words and prayers express our filial mourning: Our grief over death is great and we resolvedly perform the ancestral sacrifices." White lanterns are hung outside of the house. Inside, there are fresh daily offerings of incense, flowers, and foods on the family altar table. An image of *Co-su-kong*, the major village god, is borrowed from the village temple, and if the family belongs to a lineage that has a god figure, he too is brought to the house.

The time of burial is fixed by a horoscope expert or through divination. One item that must be specially ordered beforehand is a paper house of elaborate construction. These are burned after the burial, to provide the dead with a proper home in the spirit world. In recent years, these models have been built in semi-Western style, often several stories high, and are far more luxurious than any village home. They are well furnished, down to the detail of miniature scrolls on the wall, and small paper figures representing the many servants that the soul will have at its beck and call. One of the more elaborate ones had an automobile parked in the courtyard, a brass band, and was electrically wired so that the rooms could be lit at night. These houses are placed on display on a table outside of the house during the eve of the funeral and through the next day. Understandably, they fascinate the village adults as well as the children.

Special tents are set up the night before the funeral. The hired Taoist priests bring a large collection of scrolls and pictures which show the various courts of hell and the punishments received by transgressors. There are also portraits of Taoist deities. The pictures of hell are colorful and frightening. The top part of the scrolls portrays a judge and his assistants seated at the bench, while before them kneels a soul in supplication. The bottom two-thirds of the picture portrays the punishments the soul will receive if guilty, and for the benefit of those who are literate, the name of the sin or crime is written on the picture. The punishments are varied and imaginative; crucifixion, impalement, flaying, beating, roasting, pressing to death, and other tortures. In some pictures, the victim is clearly identified as a particular historical personage. In others the figure stands for all those who have committed a particular act: theft, poisoning, adultery (by women), lasciviousness (by men), seduction of another's wife, various forms of murder, and unfilial behavior, down to such things as cheating a customer by false measurements or adulteration of rice.

All this is quite graphic, but aside from the over-all belief in the existence of trials in hell, there is disagreement as to the fate of the soul and its journeyings after death. No villager is competent to direct the various pre-burial and post-burial ceremonies which are the province of the priests, whose directions to the mourners are rarely accompanied by any explanations. During the period of the funeral, the mourners are almost constantly on call to perform various series of ritual acts, most of which are only dimly understood.

Preparations for the funeral feast begin the day before the burial. Neighbors and hired help begin work in the afternoon and work on into the evening cutting up the vegetables and precooking most of the meat dishes. The women of the deceased's household give them assistance as best they can, taking turns beside the coffin to wail and lament for the dead. Relatives from outside the village usually arrive the day before burial, and must be served a fairly elaborate supper with wine. After supper, the women spend some time making miniature outfits of clothing for the dead (around ten different outfits) and miniature bedding, which will later be burned to accompany the soul. Other household members participate in prayers for the dead, led by the hired priests whose purpose is to speed the journey of the soul through the courts of hell. Some of these prayers are held at the altar inside the house, where a picture of the deceased is illuminated by seven lighted pans of oil and surrounded by flowers and incense. Others are held at another altar table at the doorway, or at the altar table within the tent. The people who must participate are the sons of the deceased, the sons' wives, sons' sons, unmarried daughters, and the spouse of the deceased. Attendance is optional for brothers and sisters of the deceased. Other mourners are exempt. The services go on well into the evening, and resume in the predawn hours, so that the close mourners get very little sleep.

The morning of the burial, the priests again conduct prayers, some of which involve the participation of family members, but for the most part, the family and friends are busy preparing themselves for the funeral. The degrees of mourning are indicated by differences in costume. Sackcloth is worn by those in deepest mourning. Sons wear straw shoes, dark-blue jackets and trousers, and coarse sackcloth smocks that reach down to the knees, and their heads are covered with coarse sackcloth hoods. Daughters' daughters and the wives of daughters' sons need wear only a sackcloth hood and somber clothing to indicate mourning.

No funeral is complete without musicians. Even poor families hire a few men to play during the funeral procession and in the funeral tent afterward. The orchestra usually consists of a single horn player, a percussionist, and two *hu-ch'in* (violin) players. Families with a bit more money and prestige in the community usually can obtain the services of the village musical society group in return for a small payment and invitation to the funeral feast, or hire a more elaborate band. Their performance, which precedes the burial, is a musical send-off before the procession begins its walk to the graveyard.

The music is part of a larger ceremony, held on one of the village roadways or in the temple square. Several hours before burial, the mourners form into line and move to an altar set up at one of these locations. As the procession advances, the daughters and daughters-in-law of the deceased follow after the coffin on their hands and knees, wailing and sobbing, and they remain by the side of the coffin when it is placed near the altar table. The chief male mourners follow them, and then the lesser degrees of mourners. On the altar table are offerings of candles, incense, red cakes, pork or even a whole pig's head, chickens, sometimes a picture of the deceased, and an unmarked ancestral tablet. On arrival, the chief male mourners (sons, grandsons) kowtow before the altar and pour libations of wine onto the ground. During this time, the musicians groups play their set pieces. As the music continues, the chief female mourners kowtow and make libations of wine. Then come the other mourners in decreasing order of importance, all except very young children, who only bow and offer incense. Last, come friends, who offer a pinch of incense to the incense pot, without bowing or kneeling. When all have finished, the musicians play a few more pieces. Nowadays, more modern notes may creep in. At one funeral, the band played "Auld Lang Syne" as its concluding piece.

When the mourners have concluded their kowtows and incense offerings and the musical presentations are finished, the priests lead the mourners in a circle around the coffin. The mourners then begin the walk to the cemetery, with the women wailing loudly. The pace of the march is fairly brisk, and the very elderly and the very young are allowed to travel in a pedicab. There is usually a wait at the graveyard, and the mourners sit in small groups, women sitting with women, men with men. There is quiet conversation and smoking, while hired hands or neighbor volunteers carry the coffin down to the grave prepared for it and place it over the grave, still on carrying poles. When the proper time arrives, the poles are removed and the coffin is lowered into the earth. Offerings of paper money, incense, eggs, and red cakes are brought to the side of the grave and offered to the deceased. The eldest son kneels at the grave while the priest inscribes the ancestral tablet with the name and dates of the deceased. The mourners then regroup in order of their rank and are handed sticks of incense, which they in turn place in the ground before the ancestral tablet. Moving on, they circle the grave and each throws a handful of earth over the coffin. There is usually no wailing or crying at this point. The mourners wait at the grave while the priests chant prayers for some five minutes or so, and they then circle the grave three times and begin returning to the village. The workmen complete the job of covering the coffin, and if the tombstone is already prepared, they put it into place. The full mourners may circle back at this point to place additional incense in front of the tombstone.

Returning to the house of the deceased, the mourners find that meal preparations have been completed, and they sit down to eat. The meal is an elaborate one, with many meat dishes and wine, as at a festival. The general atmosphere is subdued but cheerful. After the meal, and a brief rest, some of the mourners of lesser importance leave. Those remaining still have ceremonial obligations to perform.

The postburial ceremony is divided into three parts and is led by the Taoist priests. The first portion invites the presence of the gods to witness the mourners' worship of the deceased. The names of all the mourners are read. For about half an hour the priests chant prayers. The sons and grandsons of the deceased kneel behind them holding incense; other family members participate only as spectators. The second portion, "opening the spirit road," permits the spirit of the deceased to return to the world to participate in a feast with the family. It is a two-hour service of prayers conducted by the priests, again with the family represented by sons and grandsons kneeling through most of the service. The last portion, "releasing the horse of forgiveness," is more theatrical. The sons and grandsons sit facing the priest's altar next to a table on which are placed paper figures of the dead person and some spirit attendants. On the priests' altar there is a paper messenger riding on a horse. The messenger carries letters which ask the gods to forgive the deceased for any wrongs committed in his lifetime and praising his behavior while in the world. To a musical accompaniment, the priests dance and act out the messenger's journey into the supernatural world. The performance is humorous, and despite the solemnity of the situation, it evokes laughter. The "messengers" bribe the gods with wine, and pretend to be drunk themselves. They perform acrobatic and tumbling feats. At one performance, the dancers teased the children in the audience by throwing sweet-potato shreds at them and then pretending to try to retrieve them. Toward the end of the performance they are deliberately playing for laughs, repeating their acrobatic stunts, and pretending to fall as they do so, or engaging in a mock "chase." Finally, they collect the paper figures and withdraw inside the house, and the watchers disperse. This last section takes about an hour to perform, and provides relief after the previous three hours of prayer, music, and ritual worship.

The entire ceremony is sometimes held for the dead at times other than immediately following burial. Villagers feel that such a ceremony should be held for every person who dies, but the expense prevents some families from doing this until a later date, when they can combine the ceremony for several kinsmen.

As suggested earlier, the fate of the soul after death is not clear in the minds of the villagers. Generally, it is believed that for a period after death the soul wanders around aimlessly in the vicinity of its former home and must be fed, offered incense and money, and shown that the family is in sorrow. Ten days after death, the soul crosses the bridge into hell to face various ordeals, finally to be released into heaven or sent back to earth again. A person who has lived an evil life may be reincarnated as an ox or dog, or as a person of lowly status with a miserable life. If the family can afford it, there are ceremonies additional to the one described above, which can rescue the soul from hell and guarantee it a better future, through offerings of petitions, wine, incense, and paper money.

Burial is only a small part of the total of obligations that kinsmen have toward each other. The soul continues to exist after death. It faces ordeals far worse than those it suffered in life. It becomes the responsibility of the living to rescue the soul. To some degree this is done for the protection of the living, for there is always the shadowy thought of venegence from an "angry ghost." To some degree it represents an aspect of filial piety, continuance of aid and succor to aged parents. Finally, it is an assurance to the participants that the same will be done for them some day so that they will in turn be rescued from the ordeals of hell.

The ceremonies also make a statement about human nature and the propensity for evil. They assume that few are guiltless of some wrongdoing. The average man cheats, lusts, lies, and may be drawn into more serious crimes. Yet he is not wholly evil, for even while he commits immoral acts, he also does good acts in his lifetime. These must be remembered and cited so that the gods will take pity and intervene to rescue the soul from the punishments decreed for it.

The courts of hell, like the law courts of traditional China, deal out harsh punishments and concentrate on the crime itself rather than weighing all of the acts a person may have committed during his life. In these supernatural courts, the thief is punished for his thefts; it does not matter that he was a good parent, a filial son, a devout worshipper of some god, or a donor to charity in his old age. However, the courts of hell, like the law courts of traditional China, are also susceptible to bribes. The guardian ghosts at the gates of hell hold out their hands for money just as the gatekeeper of the local government office would have done. Supernatural beings have some of the same weaknesses and faults as humans; man cannot avoid evil doing, and neither can gods and spirits. They can be bribed with money or they can be muddled with drink, so the living have means of influencing the supernatural world and rescuing their dead kinsmen by capitalizing on these weaknesses.

The postburial services reassure the living that retribution for their earthly sins is not inevitable as long as there are loyal family members who will make the effort to intervene on their behalf. Moreover, they are reassured that the attention they pay to the gods will be taken into account after their souls are released from hell. They will not have to wander in limbo—the gods they worshipped in life will aid them in their entry into the Western "paradise", and, lest the gods have poor memories, their relatives will be there to remind them of the devoutness of the soul in life.

Yet despite the assurance of rescue through the efforts of one's kinsmen, the funeral rites also place stress on the need for moral behavior during one's lifetime. There is always the danger of failure to rescue the soul from hell, or perhaps one's kinsmen are too poor or do not care enough to follow the elaborate round of ceremonies to assure the rescue. There is as well the note of a higher morality in trying to lead the good life even though there are ways of avoiding punishments for a bad life. Morality becomes an end in itself: a set of ethical principles to be followed for their own sake, a code for human relationships that stands by itself.

4

Family, Household, and Lineage

Arranging a Marriage

ALTHOUGH THE OLDER PEOPLE insist that the majority of marriages are still arranged and carried out in traditional ways, the trend is toward marriages based on mutual attraction and consent. Parental approval is still required, and the family may present a facade that suggests that a traditional marriage is taking place, but the young people now play a more active part in the decision making. There have been a number of small changes in the wedding procedures as well.

Ideally, marriages are arranged by families, not by individuals. When parents feel it is time for their son to marry, they call in a traditional matchmaker. If the parents already have a girl in mind, they hint to the matchmaker that negotiations be started with the girl's family. Theoretically, the young couple play no part in these arrangements, and are rarely consulted. As filial children, they rely on their parents to make the correct decision, and they do not expect to see their prospective spouse until the day of the wedding.

The suitability of the match is decided by matching the horoscopes of the two young people, either by consulting a specialist in the city or by presenting the horoscopes at the village temple and soliciting an opinion from the village gods. If the answer is favorable, the families begin negotiations in earnest, with each stage in the negotiations marked by an exchange of gifts. The engagement is formally marked by an exchange of rings as well as the sending of a small sum of money to the girl's family. If the girl's family has wealth, the boy's house also sends some ceremonial cakes; if her family is poor, this is usually ignored. The matchmaker receives her first fees at this point: about $60 NT from the boy's family, and $40 NT from the girl's family.

The money sent to the bride's family at the time of the formal engagement is used to purchase dowry items. Thus, it is not really a bride price because the young couple receive it back again in the form of household goods and clothing that maintain them for the first few years of their marriage. The girl's family is expected to contribute at least that amount to the dowry, to purchase ornaments for the groom's female relatives and some small gifts for the boy's household at the time of the wedding, and to make a cash present along with the dowry presentation.

Further gifts come to the girl's house at the time of fixing the actual wedding date. This is done in consultation with almanacs to find a day propitious for weddings, with a further check on the day by consulting the gods in the village temple and casting divining blocks. The matchmaker again receives payments from both households for her help in this. Her final payment comes on the day of the wedding, at which time she receives $100 or $200 NT from the boy's family, and a lesser sum from the girl's family. In some cases the matchmaker is a relative or friend and considers it improper to accept payment. The matchmaker then takes a "red envelope," as a token, and returns the enclosed money.

The boy's family may spend up to $30,000 NT for gifts and a wedding feast, and the girl's family may spend twice that amount to provide an impressive dowry. The pressure to make a good showing explains why so many village families are willing to let their daughters work at factories and shops in the city for several years prior to marriage. If the girl "banks" her earnings, her efforts will provide half of her dowry expenses. One of the village girls was very highly spoken of because she had been saving money toward her dowry since the age of 12. When she married at the age of 22, she had an impressive array of goods rivaling that of much wealthier families.

In the past, the couple did not meet before or during the engagement period, or at least they were not supposed to. Ideally, they were strangers until the wedding day. This is rarely true anymore, and even in more traditional times, it was not universally true. Fully one-fourth of the married women of K'un Shen were born and raised there. Many knew their future husbands by sight and reputation. In some cases they had played together as children. Another one-fourth are drawn from one particular neighboring fishing village. The continual drawing of brides from this community over the centuries has set up a complex network of family ties at all generation levels. In a number of households, the women of the younger generation bear the same surname and come from the same village of origin as their mother-in-law or other older women in the husband's household or close kin group. In a few cases, the bride is a cross-cousin (mother's brother's daughter). The visiting by married women to their village of origin, taking their children along, gives the young people a chance to see each other and converse together during their childhood and early teen years.

Almost all of the other married women in the community come from fishing villages located within 10-miles distance. This made it possible for the man at least to catch a glimpse of his future bride, and several men admitted going to the girl's village to "sneak a look" before the wedding, often with the cooperation of the matchmaker. However, this subterfuge is no longer necessary. Families more and more are coming to accept the Japanese custom of the *miai* or arranged meeting, in which the young couple have an opportunity to meet prior to the setting of any formal engagement. The custom became popular in the 1940s and has increased in popularity since then as a compromise between the traditional marriage arrangement pattern and what K'un Shen understands of marriage arrangements in the Western world. For many of the villagers, the *miai* is what they have in mind when they talk about "modern marriages." A go-between is still used to sound out the families and collect the horoscopes for examination. If they match, the go-between then arranges a meeting for the young couple, together with their parents or some older relative. The *miai* takes place at the girl's home, or in a public place such as a city amusement park, a movie house, or a restaurant. The *miai* is fairly brief, two hours at most, and the conversation is carried mainly by the go-between and the adults present. The subject of marriage is not discussed—this would not be considered good form. The young people exchange a few words and observe each other. After the meeting, they are free to express their opinions to their parents and the go-between. If there are objections, the negotiations can be tactfully terminated at this point. Otherwise, the negotiations proceed; a formal engagement is set and gifts are exchanged, as in a traditionally arranged marriage. However, during the period of engagement, the young people are allowed to see each other, in company or alone, and get to know each other better. Once rings are exchanged, the boy may visit the girl's house, take her for a walk, invite her to the movies, or take her to some public place of entertainment. Some sexual activity may also take place, and though this is not openly permissible, sexual relations during the period of engagement are not regarded as a serious offense. An engagement is difficult to break, and the couple are regarded as almost married, so there is little moral censure.

However, a couple who are seen together publicly and who are not formally engaged *are* exposed to censure. The girl's reputation may be seriously damaged by this and her marriage chances spoiled. The love match is not unknown among the older generation, but it is just now becoming acceptable. Most marriages are traditionally arranged or of the *miai* type, or give the appearance of being something other than love matches. The younger generation is, of course, far more receptive to the idea of a love match. The idea has been presented to them through movies, or stories in popular magazines, or even some of the traditional vernacular literature. They are aware that love matches are the norm in the Western world, and frequent in Japan.

Several traditional restrictions on marriage alliances are still observed, whatever the mode of arranging marriages. Surname exogamy is still the rule. Even if there is no traceable relationship, it is felt that people of the same surname should not marry. In one notable instance, two young people from different Ch'en lineages declared themselves in love and determined to marry. They were persuaded to wait until the boy finished his army service. During that period, it was "discovered" that the girl's paternal grandfather had actually been born into a family named Lin and given in adoption to a family named Ch'en. The girl's rightful name, therefore, was Lin, and the marriage was sanctioned by both families.

Marriages with recent Mainland emigrees are looked down on and discouraged. Most parents disapprove, fearing that these men already have wives elsewhere and their daughters will be mere concubines. Or they fear that their daughters will be deserted if the Mainlanders return to China, or that their daughters will be taken far away and they will never see them again. Marriage to members of the various aboriginal tribal peoples of Taiwan are also frowned on, but this is a less real problem since the villagers rarely or never come into contact with members of the tribal groups. One village family, whose son suffered from mental illness, arranged a marriage for him with a girl who was part aborigine, but only after a first marriage to a Taiwanese girl ended in divorce.

These considerations aside, there is disagreement between the generations as to the proper way of arranging a marriage. The situation can end tragically. In one case, a young girl committed suicide because of parental objections to her choice of a spouse, and in another, a married girl returned home after one month of marriage and killed herself, due to her deep disappointment in her husband, who was physically handicapped. Suicide generally is a rare occurrence, but it is used as a last resort by those who cannot move authority. Sometimes it is used as a threat to sway authority, since suicide causes a household to lose face.

Some couples marry despite parental opposition. They move away from the village and break with their families. Because of the threats of suicide or separation, the parental generation is beginning to accomodate itself to the desires of the younger generation. They are generally well informed of the legal protections given to nontraditional marriages, and know that if the young people are of age, they can have a civil ceremony without parental participation. There is also, in some quarters, a feeling of relief that the young people participate in the decision. It absolves the parents of total responsibility, and should the marriage turn out to be unsatisfactory, all parties must share the blame.

The acceptance of the *miai* or a love match means a compromise rather than total acquiescence to the romantic impulses of the young. Some parents are now willing to let the young person make the initial choice, and then check it out themselves through friends, relatives, or a formal go-between. The boy or girl may suggest the person he or she wishes to marry and then go through the formalities of a *miai* or a traditionally arranged marriage *as if* they were total strangers. As long as their choice meets certain criteria, the marriage will take place without parental opposition.

There are many other considerations besides that of surname. The personality and moral character of the boy or girl are also important considerations. Parents fear that their daughter will become involved with a boy who is a delinquent, or that their son will marry a girl who is a poor housekeeper and interested only in selfish pleasures. The older people in the village cite as desirable traits in a girl such things as obedience, loyalty, a good temper, and industriousness. The young people, not always as practical, are often more concerned with physical appearance than with traits that will enable the girl to fit smoothly into the husband's household. The parents are quick to point out that love is not a long-lasting emotion and therefore not a reliable basis for a marriage. There is also feeling among the older people that love between husband and wife is dangerous, not desirable. One old man told me that he had never beaten his wife and that they used to talk things over together. When she died early in the marriage some of the villagers laughed at him and commented that she had died because they loved each other too much and that if he had beaten her, she would have lived longer. The traditional saying that a woman obeys her parents when she is a child, her husband when she is a bride, and her son in her old age is still widely quoted with conviction by the older people and by rote among the younger people. In this view of the marriage arrangement as a hierarchical one, love is not functional.

Another consideration is the relative social status of the families involved in a marriage contract. There is frequent mention of the idea that the "doors should match," that is, that the two families be of equal social standing and wealth. It would seem that this was usually done in traditional times, but love matches often cross class lines. Men working in the city come into contact more easily with women working in low-status jobs (prostitutes, wine-house girls, pool-hall attendants) and return home with wives who do not come up to family expectations. In the reverse situation, boys who have had enough education to get white-collar or minor government posts in the city come into contact with girls from households of considerably higher status than their own and a love match may result. However, such a man is more apt to move out of the village and set up a new residence in the city rather than insist that the wife live together with his family. At least, this was the case when a son of a poor family obtained a white-collar job in the city and became involved with the daughter of a well-to-do merchant family. At his insistence, his family sent a matchmaker to the girl's house and the match was finally arranged. He and his wife live in the city and visit K'un Shen from time to time, but his social world has changed from that of his parents.

New opportunities for work away from the village, and the availability of education which places some of the young in a class position superior to that of their parents, makes it seem likely that more marriages in the future will be contracted by individuals rather than by families and that the "matching" of families may not be a major consideration. Love matches are, by definition, an expression of "individualism," whether it be a young man enamoured of a prostitute, or an upwardly mobile village boy becoming involved with the boss's daughter.

Among the older generation there is recognition that the love match will become more and more frequent, and it has already met acceptance as long as the young people concerned will go along with observing the formalities normally associated with a traditionally arranged marriage. To quote one woman, whose son married a girl he had chosen from a neighboring household:

> The best thing is to let the boy and girl make their choice, and then have a go-between discuss the engagement with both sets of parents, arrange what gifts are to be exchanged. Then, on the wedding day, you invite relatives and friends to the ceremony, and have a big celebration.

Marriage Ceremonies

Whether the marriage is a love match or a *miai* or is traditionally arranged, K'un Shen retains a traditional marriage ceremony. The days immediately prior to the wedding are a time of intense activity at the house of the groom. The house is cleaned and decorated, and a private room prepared for the new couple. They may receive the parental bedroom, or younger siblings are moved in with others to make room for the new couple. The main room of the house is hung with scrolls bearing lucky inscriptions and wishes for the family's happiness, sent as gifts by friends and kinsmen of the household. The day before the wedding women who are kin or neighbors come to assist in the task of preparing special tortoise-shaped cakes of glutinous rice flour and sweet bean paste. These are sent out as gifts to family and friends, but people say that they are really meant for the children of the receiving households.

The eve of the wedding day in the boy's household is devoted to a *paipai* to *Thi:Kong,* God of Heaven. If the family can afford it, it is customary to have a pig and goat slaughtered for the occasion. These are later cut up by the local butcher, and although most of the meat is sold to him, some of it is sent as gifts to the bride's family and to close relatives. If the family cannot afford the expense, they conduct the ceremony using paste replicas of the animal sacrifices. Even in wealthier households, the family will use some paste animals to enlarge the amount of their offerings. Chickens, large cakes of glutinous rice, and six bowls of different kinds of sweets normally complete the food offerings. The main room in which the *paipai* is held is decorated with flowers. A special paper house must be bought for *Thi:Kong,* and on the completion of the ceremony it is burned so that he can receive it in heaven. Branches of sugarcane, symbolizing life and growth, are also used as decoration and burned at the end of the ceremony.

The ceremonies are conducted by hired Taoist or Buddhist priests, who chant prayers and lead the members of the family in worship. The ceremony thanks *Thi:Kong* for his protection and asks for an extension of that protection to the new couple. In some families this ceremony is held only for the eldest son or for sons who are regarded as being under the god's special protection.

The ceremony takes about two hours, starting at midnight. Ritual is interspersed with music and puppet theater. The village musicians are usually invited to perform music suitable for weddings and happy occasions, and a puppet troupe from the city presents a few short plays. A special meal of noodles and meat dishes is served to the entertainers and family members midway through the evening's celebration. Only members of the household and close kin participate. Distant kinsmen and neighbors are not invited.

The same evening the wedding feast is prepared. Few village families can prepare the elaborate dishes for the feast, but must hire a professional cook and his staff to take charge. Household women and neighbors assist, but most of the work is in the hands of experts. The cooks begin the basic preparations on the eve of the wedding. The final cooking comes the next morning, and most of the foods are left in the courtyard overnight, covered with mosquito wire or thin cloth.

The next morning is spent preparing for the bride's move to her new home. Some families still send a closed sedan chair for the bride, but this practice is becoming rare. Village brides now wear a rented Western-style wedding gown, and the sedan is no longer practical, for the dress becomes crushed and wrinkled during the trip. Pedicabs have replaced the sedan chair, and some families hire a taxi to transport the bride, even if the bride is only traveling from one side of K'un Shen to the other. The transportation is sent to the bride's house in midmorning, accompanied by men from the boy's family and by litter carriers who will transport the bride's dowry.

While the representatives of the groom's family are served tea, the litter carriers and women from the bride's family load the dowry onto the chairs. People from the neighboring households crowd around to watch and comment, while the women arrange and rearrange the gifts, to make sure that all the items are shown to advantage.[1]

The matchmaker arrives in time to assist the bride into the sedan or cab and to escort her to the groom's house. She leads the bride from her house, while the bride's family and neighbors crowd around to watch. The bride moves slowly, keeping her eyes downcast and showing no signs of emotion, for that would be in bad taste. The bride takes her seat, and the procession sets off amidst bursts of firecrackers. The matchmaker's chair follows second, and then the litter carriers and the groom's relatives. Often the bride is accompanied by her closest girlfriends and female cousins, who ride in the procession, but her parents and siblings do not go with her. The young boys of the bride's household and neighborhood chase after the procession part of the way and then return home.

Whether the bride comes in sedan chair, pedicab, or taxi, the rear of the vehicle is always decorated with a flat basket into which are woven the "eight trigrams" of yin-yang symbolism. This is to ward off evil spirits, and it is held over the bride's head as she alights from the vehicle and enters into her new home. Her arrival is marked by setting off long strings of firecrackers, which serve the purpose of frightening away evil spirits.

On her arrival the bride is ushered directly into the new couple's room. The matchmaker and a few female relatives of the groom join her there. The guests amuse themselves by inspecting the dowry as it is carried in. The wedding feast is set out at the same time and this soon claims their attentions.

Depending on their wealth, the family may invite many friends as well as relatives to the wedding feast. If the family has wealth by village standards, there will be 12 tables (120 people) at the feast. Less wealthy families have 6 or 8. Normally, only one person comes to the feast from households of distant relatives or friends. In the case of more close relatives there will be several persons from a household, that is, the groom's paternal uncle, his uncle's son, his uncle's wife. Most of the guests are male. The men sit at tables in the courtyard or in the main room. Women and small children eat together at tables in a less conspicuous location. During the first half of the feast, while the guests are occupied with eating and drinking, the matchmaker leads the groom to the bride's room for a ceremonial drinking of wine. After this, they emerge and go from table to table pouring wine for the guests, drinking toasts with them, and offering cigarettes. With close senior-generation relatives it is usually obligatory to toast individually, but as the couple work down to the lesser guests, they can toast the whole table at one time.

---

[1] Following is a list of dowry items carried during a wedding in a middle-income family: 1 boy's bicycle, 1 radio, 1 tea set, 1 set of bowls, 2 Japanese lacquerwear bowls, 8 kerchiefs (*furoshki*), 1 set of glasses, 4 girl's sweaters, 2 dress *chipao*, 1 shirt and tie, 1 wool coat, 2 pairs of women's shoes and nylon stockings, 2 cardboard suitcases (contents presumably, clothes), 20 hand towels, 2 toothbrush and cup sets, 6 bars of soap, a box containing an assortment of domestic lipsticks, face powder, and hand lotion, plus one bottle of an American-brand hand lotion, 2 plastic women's purses, 1 bunch of bananas, 2 pineapples, $400 NT in a packet. The list is smaller than usual, since this is a love match.

There is often a joking attempt by the guests to get the new couple drunk by insisting on individual toasts. The men's table will also play finger games, the forfeit being a drink of wine, and here guests try to get each other drunk.

The banquet continues for several hours. It is customary to serve at least 14 different dishes.[2] In addition to the wine provided for toasting, there is beer and soda. The cost of the meal is in part met by the guests. Those invited bring a small payment of money (from $20 to $100 NT) and present it in a red envelope to one of the groom's male relatives as they arrive at the house.

The meal over, most of the guests leave, except for close kin and friends of the family who have made special gifts for the occasion. The bride and groom are led before the family altar by an elderly woman specially hired to instruct the new couple in worshipping the ancestors and gods present on the family altar. She is also expected to give a few words of general advice to them. The bride is then formally introduced to members of the groom's family and their close friends, and serves tea to them.

Visiting and socializing continues well into the evening. The bride and groom retire to sit in their room, where various neighbors and friends come to pay their respects, look at the bride's dowry, and present small gifts of cash to the bride. In return she is expected to offer tea or soda, and cigarettes. The groom's friends sit and chat, and joke with the young couple. The bride is still expected to maintain her calmness and passivity. If the jokes become bawdy, she should not show signs of being upset. For the neighborhood children, a peep at the new couple is great diversion. They crowd around the windows and doorway, giggling and nudging each other. If the groom has younger siblings, so much the worse, for all *their* friends are led in and out of the bridal chamber by younger brother or younger sister, who assumes an air of great importance in keeping with the occasion. Finally, the excitement subsides. The radio or phonograph which has been blaring music for hours is turned off. The doors close and the household retires. Next day, around midmorning, the bride and groom emerge, wearing their best Western clothes, to pay a visit to the bride's household, accompanied by ten or more of the groom's male kinsmen and friends, and several of the bride's nephews or sisters who come to call for her.

The bride's family also prepares a feast. Fewer guests are invited, though the number of dishes and quality of the food must equal that of the previous day. The proceedings parallel in part those which occurred the previous day. The groom, as he crosses the threshold of his wife's former home, is presented with incense sticks and led to worship before the ancestral table. Then the visitors are seated as guests of honor in the main room, and served cups of sweetened water by one of the bride's young male relatives. This boy collects token payment from the visitors for the feast and offers the groom a dish of two eggs in broth, symbolizing fertility for the marriage. The groom and his companions are seated at tables in the main room, to-

---

[2] Following is a sample menu of the dishes offered at a typical village wedding, in the order that they appeared: (1) a cold plate of eggs, sausages, and liver; (2) noodles with pork and onions (3) steamed fish balls (gefilte fish) in a soup; (4) whole boiled chicken in broth; (5) fried fish balls; (6) pig-stomach soup; (7) fat pork in broth; (8) a soup with cuttlefish and cauliflower; (9) boiled fish balls; (10) whole duck in broth; (11) baked fish with vegetables; (12) boiled, sliced pork; (13) a sweet soup with dried fruits; (14) sweet cakes.

gether with some of the bride's male kinsmen. During the course of the meal, the groom must pour wine for the guests and offer cigarettes, and drink toasts with all who raise them. The bride disappears into seclusion with her mother and sisters. If the bride went through an ordeal the day before, the groom is put through an ordeal this day, facing a crowd of strangers whose curiosity he must bear with calmness and equanimity. At the conclusion of the feast, he is introduced to all of the bride's relatives and friends who came to attend, and he offers them cigarettes again, much as his new wife served tea to the guests the afternoon before. In the late afternoon the couple and their companions returned to the groom's home.

The bride is treated as an honored guest at this departure. As the party prepares to leave, the bride's parents present them with a number of gifts: fruits, packages of candies, two stalks of sugarcane with the leaves and roots attached (so that life will have a good beginning and a good end), and two pairs of chickens whose feet are tied together with red thread (to guide the couple on their future road). These gifts are later divided among members of the groom's family.

Occasionally, it happens that an engaged person dies before the marriage. In such circumstances there is fear that members of the families involved may suffer illness or misfortune because of the actions of an angry ghost. The best way to avoid this is to carry out a marriage ceremony as if the deceased were still living. If the deceased was a woman, the family must send a dowry to the man's family, and the girl's name tablet will be placed on their family altar after a symbolic wedding. Should the man wish to remarry he must cast divining blocks to see if he has permission from his first "wife," otherwise the ghost will cause difficulties. In the situations where the man dies first, the girl should ask a god's help for her own protection, but it is not necessary to marry the spirit of the deceased and move into his home, as is done elsewhere in China.

The Husband–Wife Relationship

Divorce is rare in K'un Shen. Barrenness or sterility are not regarded as adequate grounds for divorce because of the alternatives of adoption or, in wealthier households, the taking of a concubine. In actuality, in the few households where the man *had* taken a concubine, the first wife left voluntarily without any divorce proceedings taking place and the concubine assumed the role of first wife. Though some informants said that the wife could not complain if her husband took a concubine, it is obvious that the wives do protest, short of divorce.

The rare instances of divorce hinge on illness, mental or physical. One woman initiated a divorce because of mental illness on the part of the man. In another instance a village girl divorced her husband because of his drunkenness and physical assaults on her. Generally, however, divorce is regarded as shameful. Marriages are lifelong contracts which receive the approval of the supernatural and so cannot be easily terminated. Indeed, there is no legal way of terminating them, as K'un Shen views it. Under conditions of extreme stress separation is allowable; making a legal issue of it is not.

This holds true also in cases of adultery or the discovery that the bride is not a virgin. Attitudes in K'un Shen differ sharply from Confucian morality on this subject. Few men would really ask for a divorce if they found that the bride was not a virgin. Most people in the community would not make this an issue, either because public admission would cause the family to lose face or because no one could be sure that the accusation was true.

> If he discovers that his own wife is not a virgin, the husband will feel that is a very shameful thing and he certainly will not be willing to let any other people find out. The wife will certainly not admit it and will surely say that she *is* a virgin.

If there is evidence that the girl will be a good wife, her earlier affairs are best forgotten.

> Most people can't find out, but if they do, it doesn't matter. As long as she obeys you, it's all right. You spent all that money to marry her, so you'll put up with it.

There are also the difficulties of returning the various wedding payments and finding another wife. One man stated bluntly that he thought most girls were not virgins at marriage anymore, and a number felt this was not a crucial issue:

> This doesn't matter at all. Some people know clearly that she is not a virgin, and still want to marry her. Poor people think that if a wife comes to the house, it's good, because it's not so easy for poor people to get married. Besides, some rich people also marry a woman who is not a virgin to be their "little wife."

Adultery by the wife after marriage is more serious. More people think this is grounds for divorce, but no one knew of any cases in the village in which a woman *had* been divorced for adultery. All knew of cases in which she had been beaten, but allowed to remain in the home, and all knew of cases in which the husband exacted a fine from the wife's lover as reparation. One informant even suggested jokingly that there were men who encouraged their wives to have sexual relations with other men; such a husband could then "catch" the man and demand money from him.

Reluctance to divorce the woman even when she has committed a serious breach of morals is probably best explained by economic conditions and the difficulties of raising money for another marriage:

> If the wife is often unfaithful with other men, and the husband catches them, then the lover must pay a fine. A poor husband doesn't dare divorce her because if after the divorce he wants to marry again, he has to spend a lot of money. So they are punished with a fine for adultery. But a strong-willed and wealthy man would divorce her.

Some might simply tell the woman to leave and go to her lover, presumably without undergoing formal divorce proceedings. In such a situation, they would ask for financial reparation from the wife's lover. The sums range from $2000 to $5000 NT.

Within marriage, discussion of sexual relations is still a taboo topic, even among the younger couples. Many people, at all generational levels, believe that sexual relations are enjoyable only to males and that women simply endure them as one of their duties. According to this view, women who enjoy or actively seek sexual relations are either immoral or abnormal or both. The occurrence of the "Victorian" view is not unique to K'un Shen or to Taiwan. It is a traditional Chinese attitude. The good woman is passive. Generally, the husband is the initiator of the sex act. It is assumed that wives will comply, unless they are menstruating. Sexual relations with a menstruating female must be avoided because they are polluting, and the woman will indirectly inform her husband that he cannot approach her. If she is tired or ill, she will apologize to him and ask to be excused. During pregnancy and for a month following birth, sexual relations are not permitted because they are felt to endanger the health of all concerned.

According to Confucian teachings, the husband-wife relationship is subordinated and underplayed in comparison with other household ties. A man continues his primary allegiance to his parents and brothers, and the wife's loyalties are dispersed among parents-in-law, husband, and children. However, in many K'un Shen households there are no resident parents-in-law, and even in those families which are organized as stem families, the authority of the eldest generation is seldom overriding. Much also depends on the individual personalities concerned, so that there is considerable variation in the tenor of the husband-wife relationship. In some households the husband rules through fear, while in others, one finds considerable affection and understanding between husband and wife.

Thus, a number of women admitted to the interviewer that the person they were most afraid of was their husband:

Now I'm not afraid of anybody. Before my husband died, I was most afraid of him because when he got angry he would scold very loudly. When he came home, if the food wasn't yet ready I would have to run and prepare it to prevent his getting mad.

In other households, women manage to achieve a closeness with their husbands and will admit their fondness for him, a fondness which is reciprocated. They feel that he understands them and that they can speak freely to him. Husbands similarly feel that they can confide in their wives:

When I'm unhappy about something, I can't talk about it to friends, but I can talk with my wife, so my wife understands me the most clearly of anyone.

Confiding in friends is frequent, but there is fear that friends will talk out of turn and cause gossip and ridicule. Moreover, there is little feeling that women are intellectually inferior—a man turns to his wife for advice at times partly because she is equally concerned with the things facing him and partly because she may be able to suggest what to do. Very few men would go to their brothers to confide their worries or ask advice. They may consult a parent, but more likely they will turn to their wives.

Married couples also turn to each other for recreation and companionship. Unless a recreational trip to the city is specifically for the purpose of visiting a wine-house or the red-light district, the village men will take their wives and some of the children along with them. Evenings, there are conversations between husband and wife about the events of the day and family matters, or there may be quiet listening to the radio.

Sexual joking or shows of affection do not take place in the presence of others, be they family members or outsiders. However, when there are visitors to the house, the wife is not expected to fade into the background and be silent. She may retire briefly to the kitchen to prepare some snack, or run to the nearest store to purchase soda for the guests, but on her return and after she has served them she usually joins the group. She may be barred if it is specifically a private matter, but ordinary visits and social events are something in which the women are allowed to participate.

With fully one-fourth of the village wives deriving from the village itself, and another fourth coming from a village that is within easy walking distance, women seem to gain some advantage vis-á-vis their husband and his family. Their own kinsmen are close enough so that they can interfere should the woman complain of mistreatment, and many women have a circle of friends and relatives living within the community. In a village where community opinion is important, the women's friendship and kinship ties into neighboring households are a lever by which they can exert control on their husband's behavior toward them.

The increasing amount of education as one moves down the age scale also gives a woman an advantage over her mother-in-law as compared to earlier times. Few women in the elder generation have any education at all, but among middle-aged and young wives there is increased literacy. Some mothers-in-law are feared and dreaded for the scoldings they give, but they are apparently in the minority. Generally speaking, elderly women do not exercise much authority over their married sons or their son's wives, even when living in the same household. If the wife has some education, she has little trouble having her own way. Indeed, a reverse situation may occur in which the elder woman is somewhat afraid of the younger. I have heard one young woman half tease, half threaten her mother-in-law by telling her that in "modern countries" like America old women live alone and are not cared for by their sons.

The Household

The households in K'un Shen tend to be small, usually organized as nuclear or stem families. This is in part a result of economic circumstance and in part the working out of values and attitudes surrounding household and family. The complex extended family is known and occurs in the community. For some families it is an ideal that cannot be realized, and for others it is neither the reality nor the ideal.

The household is a unit for economic cooperation in which the income of various members is pooled and shared. It is the unit which eats together. Authority lies with the male head, but many decisions are arrived at jointly through discussion between the adult members. The household also functions as a religious unit, maintaining an altar table where offerings are made to ancestors of the male head and to one or another of the gods in the total pantheon favored by the particular household. It is the minimal unit which presents food offerings to the village temples at festival times, and finally, it is the unit wherein new members are socialized and disciplined.

Size, complexity, and degree of autonomy of households vary. The size ranges from the minimal 1-member household to the 19-member, largest single household in the village. Average size, however, is 6.6 members, with three-fourths of the village households having between 4 and 9 members. Size of the household does not clearly indicate the degree of complexity of organization. With improved health standards it is not uncommon to find 5 or 6 surviving children in a family, and one village family struggled to support 13 children. A large household may still be a nuclear family.

Residence patterns must also be kept distinct from complexity of organization. In some instances, a single building holds several households, while in other instances, the building holds a large extended family or one nuclear family.

The majority of villagers live in households of nuclear families (a married couple together with their unmarried sons and daughters); or variants on the nuclear family: a married couple without children, or a widow with unmarried children; or in stem families. Families whose income stems from a shop, farm, or fish pond tend to be more complexly organized than those engaged in fishing or small trade.

However, there are exceptions, for some fishermen's families are complexly organized, and there are instances of merchant families or pond owners who live in simply organized families. Moreover, the term "complex" requires some explanation and qualification.

For example, there is a compound which houses what might appear at first glance to be seven separate households. Though they recognize kin ties and jointly commemorate a common ancestor who was grandparent to the males of the eldest generation in the group, there is no one recognized head in authority over all of the units. Each unit has its own living quarters within the four buildings that make up the compound. Each takes its meals separately from the others. There is some economic cooperation in that they jointly own a large beach-seining net. Otherwise, work is diversified. One unit owns a general store. A second owns a drug shop. A third holds title to a fish pond. Those in the younger generation hold civil service jobs or white-collar city jobs. Except for the income from the seining net, there is no sharing of economic resources. However, there is cooperation in ritual matters, and in education of the young. A member of the senior generation, by virtue of his education and general standing in the community wields de facto authority without being the official family head.

Such an instance presents on the surface an approximation of the Confucian joint family, but in reality it is a loose confederation of household units. In K'un Shen, adult males expect to become family heads soon after they have married or produced a son. While lip service is paid to the idea that brothers should maintain a joint household, there is no stigma attached to household division and the taking on of authority by each brother in his respective household. The division is more social than spatial; the new "household" may be set up in the next room or a wing of the former house, and members continue to meet and sit in the same central room, share the same courtyard, and use the same kitchen (the latter can be circumvented in good weather by using portable charcoal stoves). Each acting head functions independently. He remains on good terms with his brothers and may consult them for advice, but his decisions are the final ones vis-à-vis his own household affairs.

A high frequency of nuclear-family households has been noted by other writers on Chinese rural society, and some have sought to explain this frequency in terms of demographic factors, that is high infant mortality leading to the survival of only one mature son per family, or by migration factors. While this explains some of the nuclear family households in K'un Shen, it does not explain all of them. There are a number of instances in which the parents are still living, but their married sons are established as household heads, or where the parents are dead and the sons live in separate households. In over half the households organized as nuclear families, the head has a brother living independently nearby. Similarly, one-third of the households organized as stem families would be more complex had not one or more sons moved out to become head of his own household. Neither demography nor migration are adequate explanations for the prevalence of small family units. Rather, they appear to result from a combination of economic expediency and preference.

K'un Shen recognizes that sons have the obligation to support their parents. Indeed, from very early youth, this obligation is felt deeply; all that the parent has done for the child must be repaid in full and more. Yet allegiance to parents is not sufficient to hold the household together, and in order to meet the demands of filial piety a compromise is effected. Thus, in some instances the household reorganizes into separate households, with the junior households taking, in rotation, the responsibility to support the parents or surviving parent. If there are three sons, each provides meals for the parent for ten days out of the month, and the parent may be more closely attached to one household for sleeping arrangements. This compromise does not always work to everyone's satisfaction. There is considerable bitterness among some of the older people, who feel that they have no authority over any of their son's households and that their presence is resented. It is not often that a man over 50 or a widow with a married son can maintain a position as houshold head. The leadership passes to the next generation and the elders become subordinates.

The occupation and economic levels of most village families provide a partial explanation for the prevalence of simple family organization. Few families own property sufficient to support six or seven adults, plus children, and few families own property that is permanent and at the same time divisible, such as land. Fishing rafts are neither divisible, nor permanent, nor are they capable of supporting large, complex households. Fish ponds, similarly, are not divisible, though they are permanent and support a greater number of people. Most families do not have a sufficient patrimony to hand down. Theoretically, each son receives an equal share in the family property, with a slightly larger amount set aside for the eldest son, who bears the main responsibility of care for the family altar. In reality, the father often bequeaths his pond or raft and fishing equipment to one son, while the other becomes a fish trader, or a hired worker on someone's raft, or goes into temporary partnership with a friend and borrows money to purchase another raft. If the household elders are forceful personalities, they may succeed for a time in keeping the household from dividing, but with their death it is usual for the household to formally divide, completing the process which began as the sons were deployed into different occupational lines.

This deployment in itself is not sufficient reason for division—why should not two adult men continue to cooperate economically even though they are working apart? Why could they not continue to pool their incomes? To answer this, we must consider the way people think of family unity and cooperation between kinsmen. The Confucian idea that the eldest brother takes on the paternal mantle of authority and guides his younger brothers is weak or even nonexistent. Thus, jealousy and bickering occur, especially when some of the sons do not inherit directly from the small family estate, and the tensions build to a point where any open quarrel can lead to a split. Unity does not prevail.

The antithesis of Confucian thinking was summed up by one informant who put it succinctly: "Myself first, my brothers second, relatives third." This attitude is by no means unique. "Myself first" reflects the emphasis that K'un Shen places on individual self-sufficiency with a minimum of dependence on family members. Dependence on kinsmen is a source of shame, and the Achilles' heel of the joint household. If the adult males are not making equal contributions to household income, the less productive feel shame and the more productive feel resentment. The more satisfactory alternative is to split the household.

Only a few households come close to the Confucian ideal of organization into lineal or joint extended families. Some are, as we might expect, the wealthier village families, but others are fishermen's households held together by a strong head.

An example of the former is a family whose wealth is gained chiefly from ownership of fish ponds. Here, the eldest son, now in his late fifties, is acting head over his own married sons, his younger brother and his sons, and indirectly over his parents, who are still living in the household. The compound is large, and integrated by sex and age groupings more than by units of procreation. The women eat together apart from the men, and the children eat in their own age groups. Several of the men in this family are scholars—the present head was a schoolteacher; one of his sons is doing advanced studies abroad. Such a family is closer to the gentry-family model than any of the village families. The head has political power within the village as an elected official, and as an informal leader and mediator of disputes. Economic power, political power, and education act together here as incentives to preserving family unity.

The degree of integration with closely related households varies. Even if households are formally separate, those sharing the same courtyard also share many of the problems of daily living. The women assist each other in watching the children, or in preparing some special meal, or by extending small loans for marketing. The households may collaborate on some ritual matters, such as sending food offerings to the temple, or worship of the common ancestors. The point where collaboration stops is at the recognition of common authority; despite a great amount of cooperation between households, they do not recognize one common head, and each unit is economically independent of the others.

The income of household members is pooled. Sons and daughters who work turn their income over to the parents for use or safe keeping, though usually they are allowed to keep a little for spending money. If the wife works, it is assumed that the money she earns is spent on household needs. However, income earners have more of a say in household affairs and more independence. Compared to women in farming villages, who, if they do so, work on their husbands' lands, the women of K'un Shen are outspoken and aggressive. It is their outside labor which sometimes maintains the household during the months when fishing is meager or impossible. The income of the young people is often put aside to provide them with a stake in later life. The father's authority is tempered in either case; he is not the sole support of the family and he recognizes his dependency on the others, even when he is manager of finances.

The household is also a religious unit within which certain holidays are celebrated and the ancestors memorialized. The New Year, for example, is a family holiday rather than a village-wide or lineage-organized celebration. Preparations for the holiday begin around the twenty-sixth of the twelfth lunar month. The house is given a thorough cleaning, the children assisting their mother in this task. During the holiday itself, the house cannot be swept, lest the family's good luck be swept away. The household prepares cakes of glutinous rice. Bright red strips of paper bearing New Year's couplets are pasted over the doorposts. If the family can afford it, new clothing is bought for the children, though most families are content simply to have clean clothing for the children during the holiday period.

On New Year's Eve, the household feasts. Rice is eaten, rather than sweet potatoes, and there are also noodles (for long life). Fish, chicken, and pork round out the meal, together with vegetables. Before the family eats, these foods are offered to the ancestors on the ancestral altar in the central room of the house. The gods whose figures or portraits are kept in the house are offered meats, grain, tea leaves, and tortoise-shaped red cakes. Additional foods (or the same ones, used again) are offered at the gate to the house, where the gods are asked for help in rearing the children. After the food offerings, silver paper is burned for the ancestors, and gold paper for the gods. Families who own pigs, an ox, or pigeons make offerings to the gods at the animal stalls.

New Year's Eve is a quiet time. Many houses bar the doors early, because this evening is a time when creditors go to peoples homes to ask a return of their money. Thus families pretend that they have already gone to sleep, and by 7:30 P.M. many doors are closed for the night. In the more affluent families, the doors remain open. After dinner, some of the men visit friends or relatives or join in gambling parties, or the family may remain at home, feasting and playing gambling games, with the children of the household participating.

New Year's Day is also a holiday, though in the poorer families work goes on as usual. At the break of dawn, strings of firecrackers are set off at each household, signaling the start of the new year. If the family can afford it, there is continued feasting during the day. Visits are made to friends and kinsmen to convey New Year's wishes. The children are dressed in their holiday clothing. In wealthy families they are given $10 NT apiece as spending money by their parents, and there is usually additional money forthcoming from grandparents. In ordinary families, the child is more likely to receive only $2 or $5 NT.

New Year holidays provide an excuse for a household excursion. Among the wealthier families it is customary to take the children into the city to sightsee. There, the streets are crowded with people in their holiday best, and there is enjoyment in just walking around and looking at the other holiday-makers. In the city, the holiday continues for several days, with the shops closed completely or open only part of the day. In K'un Shen, things return to normal the day after New Year's Day. Farmers and city folks may be able to take a rest at this time of the year, but for fishermen the holiday comes in the midst of their busy season.

The ancestors are included in the New Year festivities, and in a sense they are always present in the household. Every morning and evening incense is lighted for them, the task usually falling to the wife or one of the sons. There are always some food offerings present on the altar, such as cookies or fruits. On any holiday or special feast day the ancestors are invited to participate. They are also notified of births, deaths, and weddings occurring in the household but the "cult of ancestor worship" is not highly elaborated. Generally, ancestors are not remembered past the third generation: The family commemorates the birthday and death date of the head's parents, paternal grandparents, and great-grandparents in the male line. Beyond that, all ancestors are lumped together and given token offerings at New Year, at Ch'ing Ming, and at the Ghost Festival in the seventh lunar month.

In many households, ancestor shrines of Japanese origin take the place of the large wooden ancestor tablets traditional to Chinese culture. According to informants, the Japanese had a campaign early in the days of colonial rule in which they ordered the use of shrines and had the ancestral tablets burned. Whatever the reason, use of the shrines is widespread. These are boxes about 8 inches high, 4 inches wide, and 2½ inches deep. Inside them are stored tiny wooden plaques, in dimensions about 5 inches by 1 inch, on which are written the name, birth date, and date of death. Some villagers say that the use of shrines is "more convenient" or that they are more attractive than ancestral tablets. A few households have had Chinese-style tablets made recently.

In some instances it is necessary to go to a relative's house in order to commemorate the anniversary of a grandparent or great-grandparent, but this can be circumvented by casting wooden divining blocks to gain approval and then making replicas of the plaques for storage in one's own household shrine. Thus, each household is able to retain its autonomy, even in the matter of commemorating an ancestor shared with other households.

There is a certain casualness about ancestral memorials. Often some of the plaques in the shrine are ignored. In one household, for example, only the death anniversaries of the head's mother and father were observed with regularity; those for paternal grandparents and great-grandparents were sometimes observed, but usually forgotten, though the dates were known. Another household, which had a large ancestral tablet inscribed with 14 names and their dates, said that they observed only the death anniversaries for the head's father and paternal grandfather. In some households, only the head's parents are remembered—this seems to be the minimum, as no one admitted to ignoring ancestral memorials completely.

Ancestors are honored again at Ch'ing Ming, which in K'un Shen is always held on the third of the third lunar month. At that time, some of the household members (usually the women and children) visit the graveyards bordering the village in order to clean the ancestral graves and present food offerings, incense, and paper money. In other parts of China, this holiday is the occasion for a family "picnic" at the graves, but here, it takes the form of a brief pilgrimage. The foods are then brought back home, to be consumed in the evening by the household members. Usually, only the graves of the head's parents and paternal grandparents receive attention. Villagers who have moved from the village are expected to return on this day in order to visit the family graves.

During the seventh lunar month, when it is believed that the gates of the world of the dead are opened and the spirits roam the earth, food, wine, incense, and paper money are again offered to the ancestors. This comforts them and prevents them from turning into angry ghosts who can cause harm to their living descendants or to humans who cross their path.

The Lineage

Beyond the household lies the patrilineage or *tsu* (in Taiwanese, *co*). Although the population of K'un Shen derives from an area of China where *tsu* organization and functions are highly elaborated, the *tsu* here function mainly as religious cults, which have become potentially open to those outside of the descent system—membership is not strictly limited to those tracing descent from a common ancestor.

Ancestral worship is not a concern of the *tsu*, though it is elsewhere in China. None of the *tsu* in the village keep genealogical records. The closest approximation are the lists of member households and their living constituents. Nor do the *tsu* maintain halls for storage of ancestral tablets. They own little property at all. Property, if it exists, consists of a god figure, representing the patron god of the group, along with a few items for his altar such as an embroidered cloth or candlesticks. These items are moved periodically, the members households casting lots to see who shall have the honor of housing the god for six months or for the coming year. None of the *tsu* owns land, ponds, or other economic property, other than the loan funds referred to earlier. There are periodic meetings of the *tsu*, but these meetings are not limited to the males of the group, nor are they a group commemoration of the ancestors. Men, women born into the group or married to a member, and children all participate in the celebration for patron god at these times. In content and form, these meetings differ little, if at all, from cult gatherings for Taoist or Buddhist gods, or from the ceremonies held at the village temples in honor of the gods' birthdays. They are in the same pattern, the main difference being that recruitment of participants is heavily dependent upon kinship lines. As at other religious festivals (described in detail in the chapter dealing with religion), the members bring food offerings to the god and hire specialists connected with the village temple to chant prayers and invitations inviting the supernatural world to participate in the feast. An opera troupe or puppet opera is hired from the city to perform at the festival, and in some of the *tsu* there is a shaman or *tang-ki* who speaks and interprets for the god, answering questions that are posed by the members.

The largest *tsu* in the community has 150 member households. Because of size, the festival for their protector god is held twice yearly, thus making it possible for more families in the group to have the chance to house the god. Housing the god is regarded as an honor and privilege which will bring increased well-being to the host household.

The god is in no way an ancestor to the group; indeed, the names of the founding ancestors are no longer remembered. According to lineage tradition, the god, *Cu-ling-kong* protects people and rescues them from danger. He was once human, a high-ranking official whose kindness and humanism earned him the gratitude of the people, the hatred of his fellow officials, and, eventually, a death sentence from the Emperor. It is believed that he was an official in charge of migrations to Taiwan or else a guard over a group of prisoners of their surname who were exiled to Taiwan. Some reject this story and say that the god is much older and was brought as a patron when the original ancestors of the *tsu* migrated to Taiwan.

Because the god is not a lineage ancestor, some of those who participate in the celebrations come from other lineages. They believe that the god's protection extends to all who believe in him and do him homage. Moreover, anyone can come to watch the opera performances presented in honor of the god, and these always attract a large crowd. However, those outside of the lineage are not eligible to borrow money from the loan fund—a sum of money which stands at about $7000 NT.

Money from the *tsu* fund is also used to defray the cost of the celebrations and the cost of housing the god. If the family chosen by lot to house the god is fairly well off it is expected that they will shoulder the cost of inviting an opera troupe (a cost of between $2400 and $2800 NT a day) and will be given some $1200 NT in partial reimbursement. It is assumed that during the year they will provide adequate food offerings on the altar. Should the family selected be relatively poor, they are allowed to invite a puppet opera rather than a real opera troupe, and they are given between $800 and $1000 NT from the fund to pay for this and the daily altar offerings. As a result, poor households are able to receive the benefits of membership without having to go into debt in order to meet their obligations.

The second largest *tsu* in the village bears the same surname and numbers around 50 member households. Their patron god, who is also drawn from the folk pantheon, has a *tang-ki,* selected by supernatural sign from among the member families. Another member serves as his interpreter, since the pronouncements of the *tang-ki* are usually unintelligible. He too is selected supernaturally. The present *tang-ki* is a man of late middle age who has served in this role for some 15 years. By his own account, he became a *tang-ki* involuntarily. He had gone to watch an opera performance on the occasion of the god's birthday, and while there became ill. He took to bed and remained ill for several days, herbal medicines producing no effect. Finally, the god figure was brought to his home, and at that time he became possessed by the spirit of the god, a sign that he was selected to act as his *tang-ki.* He received no formal training for the role. Rather, he was taken to the house where the god was kept, and remained there for a month, gaining instruction directly from the god. Since that time, he has performed as *tang-ki* both at lineage celebrations and at request in private homes. He receives a token payment for this service, but the major part of his income still comes from fishing.

A visiting puppet show on a sunny winter afternoon.

The shaman role demands the ability to go into trance, to perform acts which in a normal state would cause pain, and to "speak in tongues" as the voice of the god. The details vary from shaman to shaman; some are noted for the ability to stick spikes through their cheeks while in trance, while others whip their backs with a spike-studded felt ball, walk on sharp knives, or dip their hands in boiling oil. Whatever the act, there is no show of pain, and the shaman, after he comes out of trance, has no recollection of his actions.

Shamans still continue a normal life. They marry and have children; the only restriction is on sexual relations on the day before or after a performance. The man who acted as shaman for his lineage did not regard the role as an unqualified honor. He said, rather bitterly, that it made him unhappy to perform because some people in the community regarded him as "crazy," or at least abnormal. He felt that his own children were afraid of him because of his role as *tang-ki*, though in actuality he seemed to have a closer relationship with his children than many in the community. At times he tried to avoid giving a performance, but the pressure from other families in the lineage was always too great.

The shamanistic performance is one of the high points of the lineage ritual. Always, it occurs in the evening, after the member families have finished feasting. The *tang-ki* enters the room where the lineage gods are housed and sits meditating until he slips into trance. He then speaks for the god, uttering pronouncements which are relayed in ordinary speech by his interpreter. Usually, he calls for his spike-studded ball and beats himself with it until the blood flows. The faithful wipe off the drops of blood with special yellow paper, later folded into amulets to be worn by the children as protection. The interpreter, on behalf of the group, may raise questions concerning lineage matters—the purchase of ritual items for the altar, for example. Then, representatives of various households ask advice of the god concerning important decisions they must make, or cures for sicknesses that have not been helped by the more conventional methods. The watching members reflect awe and fear during the performance and interruptions are discouraged. Even the children become silent and motionless.

The lineage shaman may help persons outside of that lineage, persons who believe in the patron god of the group and come to seek his advice. There is another lineage within the community whose patron god, *Thai-cu-ia,* is also one of the minor gods in the village main temple. The *tang-ki* of this lineage is of crucial importance to the entire village since he is also the only person who can speak for the temple god. Traditionally, the *tang-ki* for the god has always been selected from among the 15 or so households of this descent line.

There was much pressure on them from the rest of the village when no new *tang-ki* arose to replace the old one after his death. The *tang-ki* from another lineage consulted with his god about the matter, and during trance became "possessed" by *Thai-cu-ia.* The latter announced his intention to leave the village forever because of the death of his *tang-ki.* The family pleaded he remain and choose a successor, and finally gained his consent. After a year had passed, with no new *tang-ki* in view, they resorted to a more desperate measure. They gathered together all of the male members of the lineage between the ages of 20 and 40 and locked them in the house where the god figure was stored. From early evening until well into the next day they remained there, praying and offering incense. Finally, one of the younger members was seized with trembling and found himself unable to speak. The others recognized that he had been chosen as the new *tang-ki.* After a time he uttered some words in the voice of the god, and announced his identity. He further announced that he was to enter the village temple and remain locked within for a period of 12 days, while receiving instruction from the gods. The young man was then brought to the temple and the doors barred. During the following 12 days only members of his lineage were allowed to enter, and then only to bring him food and water.

At the end of the 12 days, at high noon, a large crowd of villagers gathered outside of the temple to watch the new *tang-ki* emerge. When the door opened long strings of firecrackers were lit. Through the smoke and haze, the villagers watched him descend, moving slowly in a trance. Many followed his progress through the narrow lanes and crowded into the small central room where the lineage's *Thai-cu-ia* figure was kept. Here, seized by the power of the god, he called for a writing brush and paper and wrote long, obscure characters which were distributed as charms. He called for the studded ball and whipped himself, while blood and sweat ran down and his kinsmen wiped it off on yellow amulet papers. The seance lasted for almost an hour, but afterward, there were some grumblings. Some of the older men of the village pointed out that the new *tang-ki* had kept his eyes open throughout the performance, whereas the former *tang-ki* always had his eyes closed when possessed by the god. Also word got out that after the seance the new *tang-ki* had joined his family in a feast, had eaten fish, and then vomited. To some, this was an indication that he had not really been instructed by the gods, or else he would have known that he could not eat fish or meat without ill effect.

The next day, there were further complaints. During the night the new *tang-ki* had unsuccessfully attempted to have intercourse with his wife. Instead, he became possessed and ran naked from the house into the courtyard. His wife was similarly afflicted, and the two of them knelt there until dawn. Again, the feeling was that the god would have warned him. One interpretation of these events was that he was being possessed by some trickster god who wished to make a fool of him, his lineage, and the entire village. The case became a matter of public discussion which abated only after other *tang-ki* were pressed to investigate the matter through the gods they served and they presented confirmation that the young man was indeed serving *Thai-cu-ia* as patron god of his lineage and a protector of their village.

More in the Confucian tradition is a group six generations in depth. They number about 25 households and a senior household functions as the ritual center. An ancestor tablet for a common ancestor (grandfather to the head of the house) is stored there, as well as the figure of the patron god. Till recently, this group maintained ties with a lineage in Amoy. There are gatherings at New Year, on the death anniversary for the founder, and during the seventh lunar month which involve representatives from the related households. Once yearly there is a celebration of the birthday of the patron god, identified as a fourth brother to the main gods of the village temple, *Co-su-kong*. He also has a *tang-ki* recruited from the male membership of the lineage. However, unlike the situation with the temple god *Thai-cu-ia,* he is not universally regarded as important. There are about 35 unrelated households who participate in the cult. However, most people prefer to approach the *Co-su-kong* figures in the main temple, even though he has not had a *tang-ki* for over ten years.

There are a number of smaller surname groups in the village, ranging from 1 to 25 households. Most of them consist of only 3 or 4 households and are fairly new to the community. For them, unity as a group is preserved through household memorials to recent ancestors. Some maintain ties to branches of the family in nearby fishing villages and travel there to participate in ancestral memorials.

We might speculate here on the reasons for the absence of complex lineage organization and an elaborated cult of ancestral memorials. These seem to have been lacking in earlier times as well—the present situation is not the result of modernization. Lineage temples exist elsewhere in Taiwan, in communities far more modern than K'un Shen. Most individuals in K'un Shen identify with a *tsu,* but here, elements of Buddhistic and Taoistic folk religion far outweigh ancestral commemoration or glorification of the family. K'un Shen never had a resident scholar/gentry class, and the village did not produce scholars, officials, men of renown, or of great wealth whose descendants would strive to keep their memory alive. The ancestors are poor fishermen, laborers, pond cultivators, and small merchants. Filial piety is strong enough so that people look after the needs of deceased parents, grandparents, and, perhaps, great-grandparents. Beyond that, the memory fades, possibly because there is nothing outstanding to remember. They were ordinary people, as are their descendants, and they left behind no land or wealth to support lineage halls and their elaborate rituals.

On the mainland of China, the impetus to organize and maintain a complex *tsu* organization complete with halls, genealogies, codes of behavior and courts of judgment, memorial feasts by the male descendants, and so forth seems to have come from the gentry class, who also played the major roles in *tsu* leadership. However, not only was this kind of leadership lacking in K'un Shen but there is also the possibility that the original migrants were marginal members of the *tsu* in their home communities. To be a member in good standing required not only the proper line of descent but also the ability to pay yearly dues and to maintain certain standards of Confucian morality. Under the latter came such matters as chastity for widows, avoiding giving one's children in adoption and maintaining brotherly unity within the household. For the poor these standards were difficult to meet. It seems quite probable that many who came to Taiwan participated little in the affairs of their lineages at home, and the descendants of those who settled in fishing villages lacked the finances, the information, and the personnel to recreate them. Possibly, they also lacked the incentive. Instead, they developed cults around protector gods, beings far more potent than their ancestors, who would look after their welfare and shed some of their grace on fellow villagers. Not all did this, to be sure. Some of the smaller lineage branches seem closer to the Confucian tradition. For most people in K'un Shen, however, the *tsu* is a semiprivate religious cult.

5

Village and Community

Good Neighbors

IN MANY INSTANCES, one's neighbors are also kinsmen—brothers or cousins sharing the same building or a new building close by—but as often as not they are outside of one's circle of close relatives and even outside of one's *tsu*. Friends and neighbors play an important role in daily life, and groupings of non-kinsmen perform a multiplicity of tasks.

At crisis points in the household cycle—births, weddings, and deaths—friends and neighbors as well as kin are notified and invited to participate. No family, however poor, would invite only kin to the wedding feast, and every man expects that there will be friends to mourn for him when he dies. A man in need of funds turns to friends to borrow money or to organize a loan club. The harried housewife runs to a neighbor's house to borrow a bit of flour, or a little cooking oil. Neighbors' children form close friendships, and so do neighboring adults. Among the women, "best friends" tend to be women in neighboring households who are of the same generation level.

In part the political superstructure in K'un Shen bases itself on the neighborhood. Under the present government, villages are organized so that 10 to 12 households form units called *lin,* a territorial grouping with an elected or appointed head. These are in turn combined into larger units called *li,* of which there are three that make up the natural village of K'un Shen. The *lin* can be regarded as neighborhood groups, though obviously people on the fringes have strong ties into other *lin* because of proximity.

Through the *lin* organizations, labor is recruited for the variety of tasks that must be done in the village. During the winter, each *lin* must provide one person to join in the night watch, guarding the village against theft or fire. At the time of temple festivals, it is through the *lin* that households are assigned the job of bringing tables and benches to place in front of the temple, or young men are recruited to carry the gods' chair and umbrellas. Village-wide cleanups and road repairs depend in part on labor recruited through the *lin*, as well as the efforts of every household to look after the area around its house.

All adult members of the *lin* have the right to attend meetings and vote on *lin* affairs, but usually meetings require only one representative from each household. The *lin* head is supposed to be elected by the total membership, but in some of the *lin* he is appointed by he head of his *li*. He acts as the intermediary between the *li* head and the households, informing the people about taxes, police registration, the availability of welfare funds, and special matters of village concern. If a family wishes to gain admission to a public hospital or feels it is eligible for welfare distribution of flour, rice, or other commodities, they must obtain the *lin* head's aid in making the application and have it stamped with his seal and that of the *li* head as certification. The *lin* head is also expected to try to settle disputes between member families and to help keep the peace.

The neighborhood has thus been formalized into a political unit, but in actuality the *lin* may be an unreal unit based on the assumption that if one household has 10 neighbors these 11 form a discrete "neighborhood unit." Often, they do not. Where the *lin* head is popularly elected or a recognized village leader, there may be more cohesiveness, but many people would sooner call in someone else than the appointed *lin* head to settle their problems. Many people are vague about their *lin* affiliation, do not attend meetings, and are unconcerned with the *lin*. What they are concerned with is the social neighborhood, which may be considerably larger than 10 or 12 households or much smaller, and which does not have to be a neat spatial unit. Fruit-and-soda stands, a small shop, or the well in daylight hours serve as a gathering place for people of a neighborhood, and certainly everyone knows the households in immediate proximity to one's own house: who lives there, what their financial problems are, what scandals have occurred.

The people of K'un Shen put much stress on the importance of having friends. The routines of village life provide an opportunity to make a wide circle of acquaintances, if not close friends. Whereas the farmer may perform most of his work in the relative isolation of his own fields, fishermen see a great deal of each other during the day. In the afternoons, there are clusters of men seated at the beach, mending nets or waiting to go out to sea again. At certain seasons, several raft owners must come to an agreement to work together to encircle the fish—the partners chosen in these endeavors are usually described as "friends," though sometimes they may also be distant kinsmen. With over one-fourth of the village households belonging to one lineage, it is hard to avoid running into kinsmen. What is important is that it is more often friendship than kinship which forms the major bond between seasonal workmates. The work crews for mullet fishing are, for the most part, "friends" of the net and raft owners; but living in close quarters and isolation for a few weeks, they become friends with each other as well. Those who have been classmates in the village school or who find themselves traveling the same road together each day to work in the city have new bases for friendship. The women too find friends through work activities such as net hauling, oyster shucking, and peddling, as well as through the confrontations with neighbors that occur as they perform their domestic chores around their homes. Moreover, women who were born in the same village manage to maintain earlier friendships.

If you were to ask a resident of K'un Shen how he defined the term "friend," he would include in his definition the idea of someone to whom one can talk freely, without fear that certain household or family matters will become village gossip. He might also include trust in financial matters—a friend is someone to whom you can loan money with assurance that it will be repaid, and conversely, a friend is someone who will willingly lend you money when you are in difficulties. Friends are also people with whom you can relax in your spare time. In the households there is often emotional distance between members, and many look outside of the household for companionship and understanding. Adult males do not always turn to their spouse for emotional satisfaction; they seek it in friendships with members of their own sex, including sworn-brother pacts, begun in their teens or young adulthood. Women are more likely to lean on household members—particularly one of their children—but women too form ties with nonkinsmen, particularly with women living in nearby households, and in some cases the relationships seem very close. Both women's friendship and the men's sworn-brother pacts sometimes have vague homosexual overtones. There is a great deal of physical contact allowed within these relationships, and while not overtly sexual, it is still far more intimacy than that displayed by married couples in public.

Friendship is, of course, a relationship between equals. Class and education enter in as variables just as much as age and sex. There are numerous cliques in the village, ranging from giggling bands of teen-age girls to the old men who sit in the druggist's shop listening quietly to opera and grumbling about the young ruffians in the pool hall across the way. If one looks further, one finds that clique members are on roughly the same income level or in the same occupation, that they have the same degree of literacy or illiteracy. Only among the children are there egalitarianism and groupings that are truly based on the neighborhood. By the end of primary school —around the age of 12 or 13—this egalitarianism breaks down. The criteria become limited. The teen-age daughters of the two households owning the large general stores become inseparable friends; true, they live only a few houses away from each other, but it is not this alone that is the basis for their friendship. The son of one of the teachers is always seen in the company of the son of a retired teacher, and the two fathers are close friends. Again, they live very near to each other, but it is not just proximity that creates the friendship. On the other hand, the toddlers from one of the village's wealthiest households play happily with their neighborhood age-mates, including the children of one of the poorest families in the community.

The lack of "class consciousness" in childhood possibly explains the absence of formalized respect behavior in adulthood. Even though true friendship is restricted to equals, there is no converse show of distance between nonequals. People are addressed by given names or nicknames, or combinations of these together with kinship terms. The village reserves formality for its dealings with outsiders.

There are a number of voluntary organizations that play a part in village affairs. Most are linked to other institutions, such as the village school or the temples. We have already mentioned, in Chapter 2, the Fishermen's Association and the Farmers' Association. These stir interest at the times when elections of officials are held, but they are not truly social organizations. They are there with government encouragement to perform certain economic functions: the marketing of fish, the dissemination of information that may be of use in gaining a livelihood, the provisions of loans.

The parents of students at the village primary school are organized into a Parents' Association with a committee of 15 members that acts as intermediary between the parents and the school staff. Anyone who wishes to express an opinion about the administration of the school or the subject matter is encouraged to relay his views through the committee. This is considered more "polite" than approaching the school staff directly. The committee meets several times each term to discuss the various comments and opinions, and if they think them worthwhile, they make recomendations to the school staff. The head of the school is a nonvoting member of the committee. The other members overlap in part with the members of the temple committee (not by design) and tend to be drawn from the better-educated members of the community. All of them are male. Attendance at the general meetings, however, includes many of the students' mothers.

The committee of the Parents' Association also maintains contact with the city government in order to get funds for the village school for expansion and repairs. Through personal influence, they are also able to raise money from among the villagers and wealthy former villagers.

There is a musical society in the village, much less formally organized than the committees and associations we have just described. The group is an amateur one which performs traditional instrumental music at weddings and funerals and which meets once or twice during the week to rehearse and play for their own enjoyment and that of anyone who chooses to attend.

We might also mention here the numerous dancing and vocal groups which are organized to perform at temple festivals. These groups are usually composed of teen-age girls or boys and utilize both songs and folk dances for their performances. Membership is completely voluntary, and financial support comes from temple funds or private groups. There is also a rowing team of teen-age girls who perform at the boat races during the Autumn Festival in Tainan.

Some young people have also been organized into 4-H clubs sponsored by the Farmers' Association. At the provincial level, there are 4-H encampments during the summer, but none of the village youth have yet attended these. The boys activities are limited to raising pigeons and rabbits, and the girls learn sewing and cooking. There are also alumni associations, a new development. Other communities have a branch of the Kuomintang Youth Corps, but there is, as yet, none in the village.

The Temple Community

The strongest organizing force in the village is its main temple. The village temple is administered by a committee of twelve men, with the membership elected on the basis of four from each of the three *li* that comprise the village. These elections are not uncontested; usually, there are about six candidates running in each *li*. Until some seven years ago, the committee was a self-perpetuating group made up of the wealthier and more respected men in the village, and to some extent the same composition is maintained with elections. Members tend to be 40 or older and from the upper strata of the community. They are usually literate. Many of the committee members are also active as officials in the Fishermen's Association or the Farmers' Association, and active in their tsu affairs as well. In brief, they are the unofficial leadership of the village. They are the men who will be called on to represent the village to the outside world, either to the government or to guiding committees of other temples. Though the temple committee is viewed in the village as a nonpolitical organization, it meshes with the political structure. Temple needs are made known to the heads of the *lin* and *li* so that these organizations can be utilized for raising money or recruiting labor or borrowing of goods.

The village temple has wide membership. Everyone in the village considers himself affiliated with it. The temple keeps a complete list of the male membership, and every household feels obligated to contribute money to the temple when asked for it. The committee administers the contributions as well as money earned by temple property. The temple earns about $28,000 NT yearly by renting out fish ponds and river fishing rights. It gains another $2000 NT from sale of night soil from the public *benjos.* Some of the money is used to pay for local temple festivals, and some of it for repairs and new equipment or gifts to other temples.

In addition to being an organizing center for *paipai,* the Lung-shan temple meets other needs in the community. For example, the temple maintains a small fund which is available for loans at interest. However, this source of loans is less important than loans through surname associations, friends, and professional money lenders.

The Lung-shan temple is also a source of medical advice. The small chair on which *Co-su-kong* sits may be borrowed by any household wishing to obtain information on the cause of an illness in the family or the required therapy. In earlier days, his *tang-ki* was invited to the house to fulfill the same function. *Co-su-kong* is particularly good at advising on treatment of blindness and insanity, though he can be approached for consultation on other illnesses as well.

The temple also plays a minor role in political elections, or perhaps more correctly it is exploited by aspirants to political office. It has become customary for candidates to come to the temple to ask the god's support. This applies not only to villagers running for office within the village but also the political candidates for the city council and other townspeople for whom K'un Shen may cast its votes in provincial elections. The candidates enhance their image by showing belief in and respect for the major deity of the community. They also use the opportunity to do some politicking among those present.

In the view of the community the Lung-shan temple is the most important one in the village. To quote one informant on the subject:

> The temple is the center for cooperation. If we are fighting with another village, the gods will cooperate with us. Confucius was great because he taught the people to read and write and that makes it easier to teach the people the rules of government. The gods and the temple are also important to the government of men, and they give the people something to obey. . . . It is easier to get people to contribute money to the temple than to the government, to give money to the poor, for example. The temple is more respected because it can foretell the future and the ways

that people must take. . . . The purpose of the temple is to gather the people together. It is the center of the village. If someone harms the temple, he will be punished by all the men of the village, because this is public property. If he steals from the temple, it is a very serious affair, and he will be strongly punished.

Local temples are autonomous, and their ruling committees are not responsible to any outside hierarchy or organization. However, there are loose regional confederations of temples. From time to time, these confederations mobilize to celebrate a special occasion together. The main temple in K'un Shen thus recognizes responsibilities to temples in several other communities, primarily in Tainan. A temple can participate in more than one confederation, although, as will be seen later, this could be an expensive proposition.

Many years ago K'un Shen belonged to a confederation which included a neighboring farming village. Today they are on very hostile terms as the result of a feud which had its overt beginnings at a joint temple festival. The temples from both villages had sent representatives into the city to participate in a parade. When it began to rain heavily, there was disagreement over the order of procession. K'un Shen gods were covered with large umbrellas, but the people from the neighboring village had none, and so they insisted on being allowed to proceed first so that their gods would not be unnecessarily soaked in the rain. A battle between the two groups started, during which K'un Shen's major god figure received a cut on the face, and a wooden tiger on the carrying chair was broken off and fell into a pond. At this destruction of sacred property some of the villagers left to get reinforcements and the fighting continued on into the night. K'un Shen's version of the story is that they won the fight. That did not end the feud. K'un Shen soon after kidnapped one of the gods from the other temple and placed him out in the fish ponds. A representative from a temple in another area had to be called in to act as negotiator for its return. Quarreling continued over the years, and the bad feeling has not yet abated.

Participation in joint festivals is a village undertaking in which the reputation of the community must be upheld or enhanced. Thus, for example, K'un Shen owed a debt to a temple in the city which had presented it some years before with gifts totaling some $20,000 NT on the occasion of the remodeling of the temple in K'un Shen. When that temple held its rebuilding ceremony, the K'un Shen temple and others were invited to participate. Villagers were pressured to contribute in various ways, including a posting of family contributions on a public wall, until some $30,000 had been collected from them, and another $15,000 from former residents. This money was used to buy an elaborately carved altar table and brass incense burners for the host temple, for foods, and for the hiring of an opera troupe.

Moreover, the village invested in new decorations for the carrying chairs of its own gods so that these could be carried in splendor in a parade through the city streets, and in costumes for the carriers. Through the temple, and eventually through several privately organized factions, the village costumed and trained several groups of singers and dancers to participate in the parade and to perform at temples along the route of march.

Finally, to enhance the village's reputation, representatives of all 14 temples involved in this particular confederation and celebration were invited to K'un Shen for a day. Over 800 visitors were formally welcomed, wined, and dined at village expense.

The gifts, the personal participation, and the hosting of a mass of visitors more than repaid the obligations that K'un Shen had to the sponsoring temple or others in the confederation. Indeed, the level of participation was high enough to suggest that something more than repayment of a debt was involved. Compared to the city and to neighboring farming villages, K'un Shen is poor, and a community engaged in a low-prestige occupation. Yet on the occasion of this festival the village was able to function as an equal or better with the other participating groups. Not only was its reputation furthered in the outside world but within the village morale and solidarity was strengthened.

Village and State

K'un Shen is by no means autonomous, though we have been talking about it as such. Administratively, it is a section of a major city, a part of the province of Taiwan, a village in the Republic of China. City, provincial, and national governments all reach down into the village. It is because of government regulations that the village itself is divided into *lin* and *li* divisions, the minimal political units in the present governmental system.

The *li* are the units through which various governmental orders or suggestions pass before they are disseminated to the families in each *lin*. At special *li* meetings, at which a representative of each household is expected to attend, some official announcements are made directly to the people, but there are many small matters which come up, such as a special surtax or "donation," which does not warrant calling a public meeting. The head of the *li* receives the information, assembles the heads of the *lin,* and they in turn pass down the information to the households in their district.

Anyone over the age of 20 is eligible to attend meetings and to vote in election for the heads of the *lin* and *li*. However, many people don't vote, under the impression that only the head of the household is eligible. In households where all the adult members do vote, they usually vote as a block. The members of the household discuss the matter beforehand and follow the lead of the household head, or a senior member of a closely related household. The idea of individual choice is beginning to take hold, however; a few people at least will vote for a candidate of their own choice, going against the opinion of senior relatives. As for attendance at meetings, quite a few people leave immediately after the first order of business, which is the calling of the household roll to assure that each household has a representative in attendance. There is little discussion from the floor, though from time to time someone other than the head of the *li* will rise to bring up some issue, such as putting in more street lights, or building more water channels, or the workings of the village school.

The head of the *li* administers welfare programs in the village as one of his tasks. Welfare funds are given to the *li* head by the city government, and he has the responsibility of allocating it to needy families in his district. The sums are fairly small. The minimum is some $30 NT a month, the maximum, $300 NT a month for needy families. Yearly, churches in the city distribute wheat flour, rice, and milk powder through the Kuomintang to the *li*, and once in a while there are donations of used clothing. These are also supposed to be distributed according to need. Always, there are suspicions of favoritism or rumors that the *li* heads use this power in order to assure themselves of potential votes or to repay people who voted for them. Some of the villagers think that it would be better if welfare funds could be administered by a neutral individual or committee.

The head of the *li* must also present proposals to the city council; if the villagers wish to have something done (construction of a new water channel, or a reduction of taxes), he must write a proposal and submit it for consideration to the city government. Because of this, it is crucial that the head be a literate and articulate man. Great stress is placed on a person's ability to make speeches and persuade through argument. Ability to speak well is often given as the reason for voting for a particular individual. Another requirement for the job is agressiveness.

Although administratively a part of Tainan, the people of K'un Shen do not identify yet with the city. No one from the village has ever been elected to the city council, although one villager did run some twelve years ago. Council and mayoralty candidates send sound trucks out to the village around election time, and come to worship in the village temple. They also feast the village elected leaders and informal leaders to encourage them to campaign for them. The city is far enough away, however, that the ordinary person in K'un Shen has little interest in city affairs. He is interested mainly in what happens within the village, and interested in the city only as events there may affect him. The local officials see to it that some 80 percent of the qualified voters go to the polls, but there is little real interest in the candidates. Similarly, there is little interest in provincial or national affairs, except as it affects the lives of the villagers directly.

Taxation is one issue which arouses interest. Taxes on the household's property are paid twice yearly, and computed at 0.005 of the assessed value; a sum one third the property tax is paid twice yearly as part of the national defense tax. There is a similar tax based on the value of the family dwelling, and an additional tax paid separately on farmland or fishponds. In addition there are school taxes, income tax, police taxes, special levies by the army, and numerous taxes on purchased goods. Everyone agrees that there are too many taxes to pay.

Military demands from the national government also affect the village. All of the able young men must do military service for two years and remain in the reserves after they have completed their army training. They are frequently called up for a month of special service, disrupting their family life and their jobs. During the summer, some 200 of the village fishermen must report for special marine training, under the officership of the Taiwan Garrison Command Civil Defense program. The program is conducted in the village, for eight hours a day for one week. In addition to fundamentals in military training, the men also receive political indoctrination lectures. The latter cover the Three People's Principles, lectures on anti-Communism and on current national affairs.

The city is represented in the village by the four policemen who maintain the local station. Aside from collecting the household records and revising them, they have little work to do. There have been no crimes of violence in recent memory, and theft is not a problem. The only case of theft that occurred during my year and a half in the village involved the stealing of a bicycle by a boy from another village. He was caught before he peddled halfway out of K'un Shen and severely reprimanded by the village police and the head of the *li* in which the incident occurred.

The national government is represented by a small unit of Coast Guard— some ten men, though the number varies. They live in relative isolation in a house on the beach and spend little time in the village itself. The officer in charge was invited to a few village weddings; the enlisted men were not. For a brief time an officer in the Taiwan Garrison Command was assigned to live in the village. In a less official way the contingent of retired servicemen in the village represents the national government.

The people of K'un Shen have been told many times via the school, mass media, and their representatives that they are now living in a democracy. Most people would repeat that if asked what form of government exists in present-day Taiwan. For most of the villagers, the definition of democracy seems to be that elections are held and there are competing candidates rather than retention of office through consensus, though admittedly there is little difference between the candidates. Some are enthusiastic about the idea that the majority decision is the one that carries. They regard it as better than a system of appointed officials, and there is some disgruntlement in the *li* where the heads of the *lin* are appointed by the *li* head rather than elected directly by the constituent households.

At the same time, there is still concern that there be uniformity of opinion and action. It is not enough that there is a clear-cut majority on an issue or candidate; it is important that others be brought over to the same point of view. Otherwise, it is feared, there will be grumbling, factionalism, and noncooperation. The idea of simple majority rule and individual freedom of choice is not widely accepted. The authority of the elders or the pressure of one's peers is still crucial to political behavior. Many women vote as their husbands do. Within households, there is often discussion so that all members of the household vote the same way. There is a drive for consensus prior to voting or a desire to turn the matter over to people with recognized authority so that they can make the decision for the group. However, Taiwan is a relative newcomer to representative governmental procedures, and it may just be a question of time before greater individualism takes root in the sphere of political behavior. At present, even though the male head of the household convinces his wife and adult children to follow his lead in voting, he himself does not accept authority from an elder brother in another household and may dissent actively from his father's opinion.

As yet, women are not active in political affairs in the village. The one exception is the wife of one of the *li* heads who recently won a post in the Fishermen's Association. There are women representatives in the city government, a fact which is known in K'un Shen. When questioning people about it, we found that their resistance was based on the fact that there are very few women in the village who have the requisite education and self-possession to hold political office. The objections were not based on sex per se, but rather on the poor training most women have for participation in the political sphere.

The Kuomintang slogan of "people's livelihood" has gained currency in the community; the people of K'un Shen accept the old Chinese idea that a government is responsible for the welfare of its people in the long run. The attitude toward the present regime is in large part based on the perceived successes or failures of the government in maintaining and increasing the people's livelihood. Heavy taxation and military demands are seen as interference with people's livelihood, and the government's assurance that these are necessary in order to accomplish the task of "fighting back to the Mainland" and overthrowing the present government of China does not raise much enthusiasm.

Although Taiwan is again a province of China, that is, under the control of a Chinese government, it is difficult to assess the degree of national identification that people hold, particularly at the village level. During the years of Japanese colonial rule, identification as Chinese seems to have been strong. Faced with the cultural gap between themselves and their colonial rulers, the villagers saw themselves as part of the Chinese world. However, this identification has been weakened in some ways since the end of World War II. The incoming migrant groups from mainland China were different from the local populace due to dialect and regional diversity. Moreover, many of the newcomers were businessmen from highly Westernized urban centers such as Shanghai and Nanking, or were typical of the professional soldiery—segments of the Mainland population which were almost as alien to the Taiwanese as were the Japanese colonial rulers in terms of language, behavior, and values. Thousands of Taiwanese died in an abortive antigovernment revolt in 1947, and the emotional scars remain to this day. Finally, the content of the ever present anti-communist propaganda filtered through the schools and the mass media often defeats its end. Rather than rallying the Taiwanese to the government's sworn task of reestablishing itself on the mainland of China, it serves to further convince the Taiwanese how wide the gap is between themselves and the main body of Chinese society.

Thus, the villagers see themselves as citizens of K'un Shen and of the surrounding region. They see themselves as Taiwanese, sharing basic patterns in common with others of the province. They see themselves as having some relation to China's cultural heritage, particularly its classical heritage of Confucian ideology, but they do not see themselves as being fully in and of present-day Chinese society, either in its Mainland version or in its urban version in Taiwan, despite the indoctrination in national goals that the young people receive in the schools and in the army. Perhaps another generation must grow up before that identification is made.

The Religious Life in K'un Shen

Introduction

R ELIGIOUS LIFE IN K'UN SHEN cannot be considered apart from the economic and social organization of the community and the wider Taiwanese culture of which it is a part. Supernatural beliefs and rituals enter into almost every aspect of life. Nor can we neatly compartmentalize Taoism, Buddhism, Confucianism, and the folk underlay of shamanism and spirit worship. The folk traditions and the literary traditions of China are inextricably combined in the total belief system. Thus, the materials in this section will simply add to that presented previously by focusing on community religious activity, the role of local shrines and temples, and the relationship between religion and medicine.

The key religious institution in the community is the Lung-shan temple. Center of the village, and symbol of the village, it is more than just a place for individual worship and supplication. It organizes the community for religious action and serves secular functions as well. The inner courtyards are used for informal conversation or games of chess. The children play freely in and around the temple. The porch and steps are often used for drying nets, for vending of articles during marketing hours, and as a place to sit and sun oneself on cool winter days. It is always open, except during the period immediately preceding the New Year holiday. Anyone may enter, provided they are ritually clean.[1]

In addition, there are a number of smaller shrines and temples in the village. There are also many god figures housed on private altars, some of whom have attracted a cult of followers within the village or even from outside the community. There are wandering gods and spirits with no fixed abode whose visits require that the community welcome them and worship them. The organization for this comes from the Lung-shan temple, since it is an affair which concerns all of those who live in K'un Shen, and the Lung-shan temple is the one temple where everyone worships, regardless of what other gods they may favor.

---

[1] The ritually unclean includes those in mourning, menstruating women, women during the first month after childbirth, and men in close contact with a birth during the past month.

We will also consider here the ideas that people hold about the relationship of human beings to the supernatural world, and their conception of a system of rewards and punishments administered by the supernatural world to living human beings. The religious life of K'un Shen cannot be discussed in terms of a fixed and systematically elaborated doctrine; it can only be seen as a totality of eclectic practices and beliefs which to the villager's mind presents an integrated whole.

The Lung-shan Temple

The first Lung-shan temple was built in 1798, and it has been rebuilt several times since then. The most recent rebuilding came in the years immediately following World War II, as an expression of gratitude that the village had been spared the wartime bombing and the cholera epidemics that followed after the war.

The main god of the Lung-shan temple is a tripartite deity known as *Co-su-kong* who is generally regarded as a Buddha and a protector of health. He is defined by the villagers as three brothers: the two eldest are in their teens, the youngest is a boy. The treatment accorded to each on his birthday is identical. Moreover, there is no attempt to distinguish between them in terms of activities, personalities, or power. They seem to be one and the same, except that the eldest *Co-su-kong* is usually represented with a black face, the second with a red face, and the youngest with a gold face. All three figures are kept in the temple during the year, and emerge only for special occasions. These may be such regular occurrences as the birthdays of each of the three gods, at which time all of them are paraded around the village, or on the occasion of funerals and weddings within the village, when a smaller figure of the eldest *Co-su-kong* will be invited to the home sponsoring the ceremony and kept on the altar for a few days.

Co-su-kong is conceived of as a protective and benevolent god who looks after the health and welfare of the community. Surprisingly enough, he is not identified by the villagers as having any particular connection to fishing or seafaring—he is not specifically a fisherman's god.

Of secondary importance in the Lung-shan temple is *Thai-cu-ia,* who is the god of the front altar. This god belongs to both the Taoist and Buddhist pantheons. He is represented as a young man, his hair done up in a topknot, and he carries a ring and a spear. In the Buddhist version he is an assistant to the goddess *Kuan-im,* and in the Taoist version a personage of great strength and magical powers.

The full-time caretaker of the temple, an old man who has no formal religious training, sleeps and eats in the back room of the north courtyard. His major tasks are to sweep and clean the temple daily and to light the incense on the altars. He plays a minor part in rituals that take place in and around the temple.

For the god's birthdays bearers are needed to carry the god's sedan chair around the community. This task is performed by teen-age boys, who also assist the caretaker before major festivals in cleaning the temple. These boys are semivolunteers recruited primarily from the poorer families in each of the *lin.* They usually have little education and for the most part belong to the group that are regarded by the villagers as *lo-mua* or juvenile delinquents. However that may be, the god's birthdays are occasions on which they are important to the community.

A more formal group associated with the temple are the *huat-su,* who are again teen-age boys recruited primarily from among the poorer families of the community. However, they must be literate since their job involves learning a lengthy series of invocations and chants of praise used during the ceremonies for the god's birthdays. A few of the boys come from fairly well-off homes. Their participation is dependent on the casting of wooden blocks to find out if they are acceptable to the god, and those who volunteer generally say they are doing it to increase the welfare of their families or because they themselves have been ill and helped by the gods. An equal number are taken from each *li.*

Recruitment to the *huat-su* group is done every ten years or so, since the membership should be kept fairly young. The only fully adult member of the group is its leader, a man in his forties, who was himself trained as a boy in the chants and rituals.

Huat-su, in addition to learning ritual chants and their melodies by heart, also learn to beat drums and gongs to accompany the chants. These young men are also considered qualified by their training to serve as future interpreters for the *tang-ki* or shaman, should the god have one. The villagers do not regard the *huat-su* as deserving any special respect stemming from their religious roles. Whatever advantages accrue to the position are personal ones; the *huat-su* can expect to live longer than ordinary persons and to have better luck during their lifetimes because the gods send spirit bodyguards to take care of them and watch over them.

Administration of temple affairs is through a lay body of 12 men, as mentioned earlier. This committee is responsible for the collection of funds in each *li,* the appropriation of money for temple needs, such as furnishings or the hiring of an opera troupe for festivals, and the maintenance of good relations with temples in other communities.

Another group linked to the temple is a dancing group which performs at village festivals and represents the community at major celebrations at neighboring temples. The group consists of 40 men between the ages of 20 and 50, drawn from the poorer and less-educated segment of the village. They are trained in the formalized sword fighting and jousting which is the main content of the dance performance.

In former times there was a *tang-ki* for *Co-su-kong,* but since his death some ten years ago there has been no replacement. People still talk about the feats of the former *tang-ki,* who could cut his forehead with a sword or splash hot oil over his hands and face without suffering injury. When possessed by the god, he was able to teach ritual boxing, and perform it well, even though supposedly in his normal state he was unable to do this at all. Since the god has not selected a new *tan-ki,* the only way of communicating with *Co-su-kong* is through manipulation of his chair, held so that it will write answers to questions being posed. Frequently, when there is illness in a household and other kinds of medical care have had no effect, his small chair is brought to the house and questions posed to it regarding cause and cure. Previously, the *tang-ki* would come in person. Chair writing is also used to determine the most auspicious dates for a wedding or building of a house, a continuation of the pattern followed when there was a practicing *tang-ki.* Many Chinese would, of course, consult a professional geomancer for these questions, but there is none resident in K'un Shen, and since *Co-su-kong* was able to supply such information in the past through his *tang-ki,* the feeling is that he can continue to supply it through written messages.

Following the lunar calendar, the birthdays of *Co-su-kong* now fall on the sixth day of the first month, the sixth day of the sixth month, and the sixth day of the ninth month. The ceremony begins on the eve of the holiday with a ceremony of about one-and-a-half hours' duration held within the Lung-shan temple. This ceremony, called *pang-ia* or "release of the camp," has as one of its purposes the declaring of martial law over the village in a spiritual sense. This will prevent ghosts or demons from committing any aggressive acts toward the community during the time that the spirit soldiers are "off-duty." The purpose of the cermony is to invite the five troops of spirit soldiers who are believed to guard the five cardinal points of the village (East, South, West, North, Center) to participate in the festivities. The symbolic gifts presented to them include straw and water, which some say are for their horses and which others explain as being for the soldiers' use in cleaning and mending their houses, and baskets of dried sweet potatoes, which are offered as fodder. These materials are all placed outside in front of the temple proper.

Attendance at this portion of the ceremony is sparse, in part because it is held within the dinner hour, from about 6:15 to 7:45 P.M., when most people choose to be at home. The only participants whose presence is required are the members of the temple committee, the *huat-su* group, and the temple custodian, who looks after the symbolic offerings. The temple personnel and *huat-su* prepare and burn invitations to the next day's ceremony which are written on slips of yellow paper. The *huat-su* group leader plays the major role, chanting the initial incantation of invitation to the spirits, lashing at the five cardinal directions with a braided rope to call the spirit soldiers, waving a sword on which is incised the Great Dipper, or using its handle to beat a rhythmic accompaniment during his chanting.

After the initial chant the *huat-su* group performs a series of standardized chants to a drum and gong accompaniment. These chants are incorporated at different points in the following day's activities and form the core of the liturgy for many other festivals held in the village. Knowledge regarding the many supernatural beings named in the chants is extremely scanty, even among the *huat-su* group, and to the average listener the chants are unintelligible due to their literary style.

On the eve of the festival, no special ceremony is observed in the village households, and unless the family has invited guests from outside the community, the evening meal consists of the usual fare. Married daughters and their children are expected to visit the village at this time, and relatives who have moved away will also use this occasion to visit.

The morning of the festival, the village square is a scene of great activity. The morning market is filled with better foods than usual and every family hopes to be able to buy pork or chicken for their evening meal. Individual visits to the temple begin fairly early in the day, so that by 10:00 A.M. the air is already thick with incense smoke. The visitors are mainly women. Meantime, at the far end of the square opposite the temple, volunteers from each of the three *li* put up the poles and planks for an opera stage. At the temple, carrying chairs for the temple's gods are brought out onto the porch and covered with elaborate embroidered covers, while individual worship inside the temple continues throughout the morning.

In the early afternoon, around 2:00 P.M., the *huat-su* group convenes inside the temple and repeats the cycle of chants. Two large pans filled with oil are set afire, and yellow invitation slips to the spirit world are thrown into the burning oil. After the prayers, one of these pans of oil is taken up by the temple custodian and an assistant. Together, they go from house to house carrying the oil and a bundle of slips of yellow paper. At each house, one of these slips, which bears a magic character in black ink, is placed over the doorway of the house and some of the oil from the container is placed over the doorway of the house. The purpose is to bring safety to the household during the year. Meanwhile, the spirit soldiers are again summoned. At the completion of the liturgy, the *huat-su* parade around the community to the spirit-soldier camps. The god's sedan chairs are carried by the boys group mentioned above, while the *huat-su* carry their drums, gongs, pottery urns, and a rack holding sticks topped with wooden puppetheads representing the spirit generals who guard the community and command the troops of spirit soldiers.

Villagers along the line of march wait outside their houses, holding incense in greeting. At each "camp," the procedure is the same; a new pottery urn whose bottom has been smashed out is placed on the ground and a stake about 8 inches long is driven through it. A red strip of cloth, bearing the name of the general in

To the beat of drums, the patron god's sedan chair is paraded around the village.

black ink, is tied around the top of the stake as an invitation. Chants appropriate to the site are sung, depending on whether it is East camp, West camp, North camp, and so forth. The head *huat-su* waves the black pennant flag to call the spirit soldiers at each campsite, cracks the whip at the five directions, and sprays wine from his mouth to the five directions to drive away any evil ghosts and spirits that might be hovering nearby. Paper money is burned at each site. The urns and invitation sticks are left at these campsites until they disintegrate. The children would not think of removing them to use as playthings, for it is understood that these are sacred objects.

The entire procession takes about one hour, and returns to the temple at its conclusion. While the procession makes its rounds, the opera starts and draws a considerable crowd, composed primarily of children and older men. Most women are busy at home preparing the evening meal. At the same time, volunteers from each *li* bring benches and tables to the plaza and place them in rows along the sides of the square. In the midafternoon, each household carries its evening meal to the square and places its dishes on one of the benches. Each family brings a large pot of steamed rice and several side dishes of meats and vegetables proportionate to the number of family members and guests who will be partaking of the meal later on. More elaborate dishes, brought by the temple committee and placed on altars inside the temple, include whole chickens and ducks, large fish and slabs of fat pork, even though the Buddhist god is said to be a vegetarian.

Each year a new *lo-cu* is selected by casting of wooden blocks. His task is to serve food to the gods on their birthday by placing a stick of lighted incense in the rice pots. When the incense has burned down, he asks the gods whether they are satisfied by casting blocks and then informs the villagers whether or not they can take the food offerings back to their own homes. Another task he performs is that of collecting paper money from each household in the village. This is burned inside the temple for the gods while they partake of their meals.

In the late afternoon, the gods are invited to eat and the foods remain outside for about an hour until the signal is given that each family can now collect its dishes and return home. At the same time, the *huat-su* group again offers grass and water to the spirit-soldier troops on the steps of the temple. A gong is struck as a signal that the soldiers of the god are now off duty, free to take supper and watch the opera.

When the gods have finished their share of the foods, the representatives from each household return home with their offerings and the family eats. On the day of the festival it is expected that each household will have guests, particularly if it is the festival in the first lunar month. It is not so much that this birthday looms as the most important, but rather that it falls within the period of the New Year holiday. Villagers who have moved away expect to return for a visit during this period in any case, and the *paipai* provides a specific date on which to make the visit.

Because it is a special occasion, most families will usually have a yellow-rice wine to accompany the meal. If the group is large enough, the men eat separately from the women and children, and where wine is being consumed, they play various finger games during the meal. Drinking is moderate, and rarely will an individual be noticeably intoxicated.

Inside the temple, women paipai *with incense, perhaps asking for sons.*

After supper, the women visit the temple, bringing their children with them to *paipai*. Throughout the evening, until about 10:00 P.M., the temple is very crowded and the air is heavy with incense smoke. There are some men present, but the worshippers are predominantly women and children, some of whom stay a long time, praying and bowing before the altars. The audience at the evening performance of the opera is even greater than the daytime one; most of the village men work, even on these festival days, but they are free to relax in the evening. The audience is casual. People chat during the duller parts of the opera, move around, and visit with each other. The children are given a little spending money to use at the visiting peddlers' stalls. Some are lotteries where the choice of a right number wins the player a piece of candy. Other stalls sell ices or sweets, and the children crowd around to buy, or just to stare. However, some of the men and boys are more interested in the events that are to take place some distance behind the stage area, away from the carnival atmosphere of the opera and stalls.

Here an altar is set up, holding meats, wine, incense, the puppetheads of the spirit generals, and the figure of *Thai-cu-ia*. The *huat-su* group clusters around this altar and chants portions of the liturgy. The leader of the group, meanwhile, lights a bundle of incense and, holding it in his hands, bows before each of the god's carrying chairs, and kowtows before the temporary altar. He then spreads brushwood and coals, brought to the site earlier in the evening, into a large circle on the ground and sets them afire. Chanting of the liturgy continues as the fire begins to die down. When the flame subsides to glowing coals, the leader and an assistant level them with a long bamboo pole and toss handfuls of salt on them for purification. The leader circles the bed of coals, waving the black pennant flag. At intervals, he throws yellow paper invitations to the gods and their soldiers onto the coals. When this is completed, the fire walking can begin.

The boys who carried the gods' chairs earlier in the day now shoulder them and begin to circle the bed of coals. As they circle, they push back the watching crowd of men and boys. They make three complete circles, while the *huat-su* leader again throws salt onto the coals, and strikes out with his whip to drive away any evil spirits. Then the chairs are carried at a run across the hot coals, circle around again, and after crossing three times are carried back to the area in front of the temple.

After the chairs have gone across the coals for the second time some of the men and boys in the watching crowd follow barefoot across the coals. A few of the men carry young sons on their shoulders as they cross, to bring them health and luck.

The chair carriers are not yet finished for the evening. As they circle the fire, it is believed that they are possessed by the spirit of the god they carry or by some supernatural being and these spirits have not yet left them. Most of the boys show signs of possession, with their eyes partially closed, their mouths hanging open, and a drugged expression on their face. The chairs they carry bounce and wave as if of their own volition. Soon, the movement becomes more agitated and the chairs are carried at a run back and forth across the plaza. They rush at one another as though they were going to collide, and veer away only at the last moment. Or they rush at the watching crowd as if they were going to crash through it, turning away only at the last moment and causing momentary panic and flight among the onlookers. Possession may continue for almost an hour before the chairs finally halt and the boys carry them wearily to the steps of the temple.

The opera continues uninterrupted and holds most of its audience during these events. After the chair procession has finished, some of the women and children return home to rest, but most of the men remain at the opera until it finishes at midnight. Those who go home can still hear the opera, carried by the loudspeaker system across the village. The *huat-su* group congregates for the last portion of the festival at the temple, where they again run through the entire cycle of chants, changing the words "invite to come" to "invite to return" so that the spirit soldiers and their generals will return to their camps.

According to the leader of the *huat-su* group, the only time the ceremonies will be altered is in the event of rain. Then, the fire walking will be omitted because of the danger that those who cross the coals would be burned. Otherwise the sequences and their components remain the same.

The opera presentations vary from festival to festival save for a short opening piece designed to honor the gods generally. Otherwise, the operas are essentially secular pieces drawn from the large repertoire of Taiwanese opera: stories about generals, officials, merchants or young scholars, without any direct relation to religion. They are meant for amusement rather than religious instruction, and it is only indirectly that they reflect Confucian morality, or Taoist and Buddhist ideas.

A typical opera would be *Lam-thi:-mng* (The South Gate), which deals with a loyal servant who makes great sacrifices for her mistress and is eventually rewarded by the gods. Another favorite plot deals with an evil concubine who attempts to poison her husband's first wife, but by mistake kills her own brother. She then accuses the first wife and has her imprisoned, but eventually justice triumphs and she is punished. The plots of these operas are well known to the villagers so that even if they cannot completely understand the sung portions or the highly stylized declamation of the dialogue, they are still able to follow the story.

The Gods of Heaven

Pai Thi:-kong is held on the sixteenth of the eleventh lunar month. *Thi:-kong,* also known as the Jade Emperor, is believed by the villagers to protect the community. He is, in popular belief, the supreme ruler of heaven. The various Buddhist and Taoist deities are his subordinates, in a hierarchy which parallels that of the civil bureaucracy of traditional China. In such thinking, *Co-su-kong* is but one of many local administrators and officials, while the Jade Emperor is the ultimate authorty.

This *paipai,* unlike the one previously described, involves active participation only from the members of the temple committee, and a hired Taoist priest with one or two assistants, who officiate. The committee represents the village, and few others attend.

The sacrificial offerings for the *paipai* are more elaborate than those provided for *Co-su-kong*. Traditionally, there is the sacrifice of a pig and a goat, which are purchased out of temple funds. To make the offerings more elaborate, wheat-flour representations of pigs and goats are added to the offerings. These are placed on large tables, one at each side of the main entrance to the temple. Other tables hold offerings of more usual items such as noodles, flat wheat cakes, whole ducks, red rice-flour cakes and various sweets and fruits. In addition, the *paipai* marks the time at which new lanterns should be bought for the temple, so that the temple is newly decorated for the occasion. Especially for *Thi:-kong,* a large centerpiece is made out of paper, representing a temple surrounded by various warriors and officials who are the god's retainers and administrators.

The ceremony runs all night, beginning at midnight and lasting until dawn. A Taoist priest officiates, while the members of the temple committee kneel behind him on straw mats and follow his instructions. The formal ceremony consumes only part of the midnight-to-dawn hours; some time is spent in preparation and in the presentation of a puppet play. The formal part consists of reading the names of all males resident in the village, interspersed with Taoist religious chants. It ends some two hours later with a prayer asking for peace in the name of the village, an enumeration of the offerings made to the Jade Emperor, and a request for his forgiveness for any wrongs done by the villagers in the past. There is then a brief recess, during which the opera performs for about 20 minutes. The puppets used are special string puppets, about 1½-feet high. The troupe is hired from the city. The operas that they perform are in another dialect of Hokkien not understandable in K'un Shen. For this ceremony they always perform the same piece, which deals with a mortal who is rewarded for his filial piety by being sent a fairy wife. After she conceives a son for him she returns to heaven, leaving him with his son.

Meantime, the Taoist priest and the temple committee check the list of names that was read to make sure there were no errors. They also remove most of the food offerings, except for the slaughtered goat and pig, and replace them with fresh ones. The priest again leads the temple committee in worship with bundles of incense, and rereads the list of names. Before they have finished the opera resumes. By early morning, the ceremony is ended and the village has begun to stir. Now the villagers have an active role to play. Each household is expected to burn paper money and set off a string of firecrackers on arising, and to send a delegate to the temple bearing a bowl of sweet rice-flour balls. The delegate is almost always a young child. The sweets are offered to *Thi:-kong* with the burning of additional paper money and incense, and then taken back home. By 6:30 A.M. the temple becomes quite crowded, as does the marketplace. The sacrificial goat and pig are dismembered by the local butcher, who buys the animals from the temple and then sells the meat in the village. On this day the family meal is more elaborate; in addition to the meat sold, there are more fish and vegetables than usual at the morning market.

Worship of *Thi:-kong* is not limited to this festival held at the Lung-shan temple. On the ninth of the first lunar month, which is his birthday, households that have had a marriage during the past three years are expected to thank him at an early morning *paipai* held at the household altar. This *paipai* is traditionally held between 4:30 and 5:30 A.M., and participants are limited to the married couple and parents.

From time to time, the Jade Emperor is believed to dispatch one of his officials to earth to patrol and investigate. In some years this may occur as often as three times, while in other years it may not occur at all. The visiting god is said to stay in the village a minimum of three days, thus allowing the inhabitants sufficient time to prepare a proper farewell *paipai* for him when he is ready to leave. When a visit takes place, the Lung-shan temple is again involved, since the brothers of *Co-su-kong* are responsible for welcoming him.

Two wandering inspector gods periodically visit K'un Shen. One is a god who travels the roads, and the other, a god who travels by sea. Since K'un Shen can be reached by either route, both gods are expected to visit. The visits are announced through a *tang-ki*. The temple custodian then informs the community, going through the village streets beating on a gong and crying out the announcement.

On the morning of the god's arrival he is welcomed at the temple with incense and candles. During the days that the god conducts his investigations, it is customary that each household *paipai* to him once in the early morning, once in the evening. Offerings of incense, candles, and flowers are considered sufficient. At the Lung-shan temple, an altar table is placed outside the doorway and the figure of *Thai-cu-ia,* in his capacity as "god of the central altar" within the temple, is placed there to welcome the visiting god.

On the day of the god's departure, preparations are more elaborate. A paper boat for his journey or small bags of rice and tiny packets of firewood are prepared by each household. Every household is expected to prepare an elaborate evening meal and to bring it to a central point to offer to the god and his attendant troops. The sending-off ceremony is usually held in the area that marks the South camp of the spirit troops. In the late afternoon, the village households bring their rice and side dishes to place on benches, in offering to the god, as well as paper money for him. The *huat-su* are present to perform some of their chants.

After casting of wooden blocks indicates that the god and his troops have finished eating, the packets of rice and firewood, wrapped in red cloth, are set ablaze in a large bonfire. Incense sticks from the various rice pots are added to the fire. As the fire dies down, the inspector god and his troops depart.

No carved image is ever made of these inspector gods, and there is no conception of what they look like. There is some confusion about their names, and disagreement over what they do during the time they are in a given community. One informant was of the opinion that the god came only to bring protection, to prevent illness, and to help people earn more money, and that he did this of his own volition during a pleasure trip. Another felt that he was specifically sent by the Jade Emperor to investigate men's activities, parallel to secret police being sent by the government. A third informant explained that while the god himself was benevolent in his intentions, the troops that followed him were a mixed breed, some of whom would bring misfortune and harm. And some felt that illness or misfortune would strike evildoers shortly after the god reported back to his superiors.

The *paipai* for these two inspector gods is, of course, not unique to K'un Shen. Neighboring villages follow the same customs. As might be expected, the visit of the god to one of these villages is usually followed by a visit to another of the neighboring villages, and before his departure from K'un Shen people were beginning to speculate which village he would inspect next.

The Spirits of Hell

Through the seventh lunar month it is believed that the gates of the Buddhist hells are open. The living are then in danger from "hungry ghosts" who died violently or from injustice or before their time, or who have no descendants to look after their needs in the other world. Such ghosts are around at other times of the year as well, but they become more dangerous during the seventh lunar month. To protect the community, the Lung-shan temple organizes cermonies.

The purpose is to feed the ghosts and provide them with money, thereby pacifying them so that they will do no harm to the living. Presumably, the only ones that would do harm would be those ghosts who emerge from the gates of hell and find no meals prepared for them by their descendants. Therefore, the community must arrange an offering to them, in addition to each household having a responsibility toward its own ancestral spirits.

The temple committee is responsible for the organization of the *paipai* and allocates funds for the various components of the festival. It is necessary that a Buddhist priest be hired to chant sutras, and lead the ritual. In addition, it is customary to hire a puppet opera for the day. Another customary item of expense is a huge paper construction about 10 feet high and 5 feet long representing the mountain of *Kuan-im*. The goddess sits at the top, and the descending terraces of the mountain hold various paper figures representing soldiers, scholars and officials, and a host of supernatural personages. This paper construction is burned at the end of the *paipai*.

The other items for the *paipai* are paid for through the *lin,* and *li* organizations. Each household is expected to contribute around $10 NT per month toward the purchase of special cakes and paper money. During the *paipai* these items are displayed with a red paper flag bearing the names of the heads of the contributing households. Thirty-six households are selected each year, by casting blocks, to be "head households," responsible for the work of putting up the opera stage and arranging tables for the food offerings. All households are responsible for presenting two dishes. These differ from the offerings made at other village *paipai*. Large tin basins are used. They are filled two-thirds full with rice or dried sweet potatoes. A sheet of paper is laid over this base, and the remainder of the basin is filled with other food items, decoratively arranged. For example, peanuts are dyed in bright colors and arranged in patterns. Vegetables are carved into flower forms or eggs are decorated so as to resemble frogs or mice. Whole fish are presented, nestling on arranged pine twigs. The village shopkeepers are expected to make a contribution, on loan, to the *paipai,* setting out a large part of their stock on a special altar. Nowadays, they pile up cans of milk, fish, and fruits, along with bottles of wine.

The presentation of foods for the ghosts is not made until evening, after supper. While the main crowd of villagers amuses itself by looking at the different food arrangements (sometimes making invidious comparisons) or watching the opera, the priest leads the temple committee members in a series of ceremonies, beginning at the Lung-shan temple and continuing around to the various other altars which have been set up.

In addition to the "hungry ghosts," the temple gods, and *Kuan-im* with her retinue, a *paipai* must also be performed to the *Hou-hia-ti,* the "good brothers."

The good brothers are ghosts who are not locked up in hell during the year. In a sense they are comparable to escaped criminals, who are potentially dangerous. The village is concerned with them at many other times during the year. They are always present, but special attention must be paid to them at the Ghost Festival. The thirty-six "head families" are responsibile for setting up a special altar to the "good brothers" with a food offering from each of them.

Awareness of the presence of supernatural agents continues in the community throughout the month. From beginning to end there are taboos to be observed; it is forbidden to hang clothing out overnight because the bamboo poles might be an obstacle to wandering ghosts. It is forbidden to throw water on the ground at night because it will disturb the ghosts. It is also forbidden to talk about ghosts and especially forbidden to say something negative about them or to them. Finally, people who seem to be having a period of bad luck are advised not to go out at night, to travel, or to go into the water of the ponds and oceans. None of these strictures is universally observed nowadays, except for the taboo on hanging out clothes overnight. This is probably because it is the most easily checked and could lead to neighborhood quarrels between traditionalists and skeptics. However, even with present-day lessened observance, the seventh lunar month is a solemn time.

The Goddess Kuan-im and Other Deities

A temple of secondary importance in the community is the small temple built for the goddess *Kuan-im,* the goddess of mercy. She was originally the object of veneration for a small lineage-based cult, but after World War II a small one-room temple was built for her. It differs markedly from the usual temples in Taiwan in that it is built high on stilts and can only be reached by ladder. Women are strictly forbidden to enter it at any time, the only exception to this being an elderly women directly descended from the original owner household of the goddess, who serves as caretaker of the temple. Though men have access to the temple, it does not serve as a social center, and it is rarely entered, except at festivals.

Since the late 1940s, the goddess has held the status of "public god" or village god, worshipped by the entire community. People believe that she protects them from illness, assures that they live peacefully, and grants prosperity. Three festivals are celebrated in her honor on the nineteenth of the second lunar month, which is the date of her birthday, the nineteenth of the sixth lunar month, which is the anniversary of her becoming a Buddha, and the nineteenth of the ninth lunar month, which commemorates the date of her becoming an acolyte. Following the general *paipai* pattern, the villagers bring food offerings to the temple at these times. Since she is vegetarian, it is not necessary to present meat dishes to her, but meats have to be prepared to "reward the soldiers," as is done at the Lung-shan temple *paipai.* Generally, the food preparations tend to be simpler. Fewer dishes are prepared by the participating households. Fewer outside guests are invited for these festivals, and the general atmosphere is less lively than a *paipai* for *Co-su-kong.* The processions of her carrying chair through the village and firewalking do not occur. Even the opera troupe that is hired seems to be of lesser quality. The *huat-su* group of the Lung-shan temple participates in the *paipai,* rewording parts of the ritual for *Co-su-kong* so that it is applicable, and summoning the spirit soldiers who attend *Kuan-im* to enjoy the feast and watch the opera.

The figure of *Kuan-im* is not removed from the temple, even during the festivals in her honor. Those who wish to pray to her do so at an altar table placed in front of the temple. This altar is bare, except for an incense burner and a pair of divining blocks, and no image of the goddess is visible to the worshipper. However, during the time I was in the village, *Kuan-im* became less remote from her public. During the course of village preparations for participation in a large festival in Tainan, she rose in importance. Members of one of the village factions entered her temple, and through chair writing divined that not only did the goddess wish to be included in the festival but that she also wished to be brought out of her temple, and paraded through the village and city streets. A new carrying chair was made for the goddess. Teen-age girls were recruited to act as chair bearers, despite the taboo on women approaching her in her temple.

Nevertheless, in comparison to *Co-su-kong,* various lineage gods, and the other god figures kept in the village temple, *Kuan-im* is still somewhat remote from the villagers. Some families have always worshipped her privately at their household altars, where she is represented by painting or inexpensive print. The figure of the goddess had not been seen for some 12 years or more by most of the villagers, since the time when she was first installed in her shrine. Should there be signs in the future that she wishes to descend from her temple at festivals or that she will permit women inside the temple, there is a chance of her growing in importance to rival *Co-su-kong.* The village men direct the ceremonies, but it is the village women who are the main worshippers and the active supplicants before the gods. Restrictions on female worshippers keep *Kuan-im* from becoming more popular in the community.

The shrine receives some of its funds through the Lung-shan temple and the remainder through voluntary contributions made at the time of the *paipai.* Arrangements for hiring the opera troupe and constructing the temporary stage are made by the head of the *li* in which the shrine is located. The caretaker is not paid for her services, and the incense offered daily at the shrine is paid for by the caretaker and members of her family. As yet there is no elected or appointed committee to administer the affairs of the shrine of *Kuan-im,* and no other group formally associated with the temple except for the temporary group of girl chairbearers and a group of five girl dancers.

Continuing in order of relative importance, the village supports three shrines dedicated to *U-ieng-kong.* These are small one-room shrines similar to many hundreds of Earth God shrines found all over the island. They represent the burial place of the drowned or other dead whose ghosts might bring troubles to the community. One temple is built over the bones of drowned bodies found on the beach, in order to protect the village fishermen. Another of the shrines was built to house someone of the village who died and returned as a malevolent ghost.

The name itself derives from a saying written on a piece of cloth over the tiny altar table: "Those who ask will certainly be answered." It is believed that prayers for success in fishing will be answered at this shrine.

These shrines are a focus of interest mainly on the third of the third lunar month, when the village celebrates the *Ch'ing Ming* festival, at the Ghost Festival during the lunar seventh month, and at times when the fishing catch has been particularly large. At those times, many of the fishermen's households send a member to offer food, wine, incense, and paper money at the shrine. At *Ch'ing Ming* it is appropriate for the worshipper to sweep the shrine, just as he sweeps the ancestral graves.

The *Hou-hia-ti,* or good brothers, whom we have already mentioned, are regarded as being in the same category as *U-ieng-kong.* That is, they are ghosts who are continually present in the village and who must be placated from time to time in order that they do not cause harm. Families engaged in cultivating fish ponds and families involved in some form of commercial enterprise are more concerned with the good brothers than are fishing families. At major festivals, and also at the first and fifteenth of the lunar months, these families are expected to perform a small *paipai* beside their fish ponds, or in their courtyard. Actually, few households are this strictly observant, except at the Ghost Festival, the New Year festival, and *Ch'ing Ming.* Once a year, at the end of the fishing season, a date will be selected, through the intermediary services of one of the major village gods, to formally thank the good brothers for their help and protection during the year. This act is tied in with observances for *U-ieng-kong* so that both fishermen and people in other occupations are involved. However, relatively few people participate and there is no attempt to make the occasion a major village festival. Again, on the fourteenth of the seventh lunar month many families hold a *paipai* outside of their homes to honor the "good brothers" with food and wine. A few households buy a paper stage with cutout figures on it which symbolize the performance of a play to amuse the "good brothers." At the end of the *paipai,* the paper stage and actors are burned.

There are a number of minor deities worshipped in the community. One is the goddess associated with the Great Dipper, who is regarded as a special protectress of children. Her birthday falls on the seventh of the seventh month, at which time it is customary to hold a small household *paipai.* The offerings tend to be simple, running to a few plates of sweets and fruits, and few households present a meal. Households in which someone is celebrating their sixteenth year of life have more elaborate ceremonies.

Some households keep a sign of the Kitchen God, usually a strip of paper kept in the kitchen over the stove and renewed each year. Prior to the new year it is believed that the Kitchen God goes to heaven to report on the doings of the family. To assure a good report, the Kitchen God is offered food and wine before leaving, and paper money and a paper chariot are burned to provide a comfortable trip. This custom is not widespread, and many households claim never to have heard of the Kitchen God and do not keep any sign of him, though elsewhere in China he is very important.

Families with children under the age of 12 *paipai* to the *Chng-bu* on the fifteenth of the seventh lunar month. This goddess is a protectress of small children. A small *paipai* is conducted for her in the parental bedroom. In addition to offering four small bowls of food, paper clothing is usually burned for her. Some households feel that it is no longer necessary to continue these *paipai* after the child is 7 years of age.

Food, wine, and incense are offered to Ong-ia. *The courtyard is decorated with a gold and silver embroidery showing the Eight Immortals.*

Small cults have formed around several gods who have been brought into the village from other locations because of their healing powers or other qualifications. One such god, for example, is *Ti-Ong-ia* or simply *Ong-ia,* who is cared for in a private home.[1] He was brought into the community about 20 years ago in order to cure sickness. The owner of the house where he is kept is also *tang-ki* for the god, but he performs infrequently. There are 20 families which form the core of the cult. Many households joined the group after approaching the god and receiving satisfactory advice. Parents of sick children bring them before the god and offer them in "adoption" if he will cure them; if cured, it is expected that the children will continue to worship the god and present food and incense offerings to him on his birthday. *Ong-ia* has "adopted" over 100 children in this manner. The children receive a copper-coin amulet and an undershirt which convey the god's protection and help to ward off further illness.

When the *paipai* is held for him, the participating families contribute money to defray the cost of the occasion. Contributions average $20 NT ($.50 U.S.). This pays the cost of inviting the temple *huat-su* to perform chants to call the spirits to the feast.

The Earth God is of considerable importance in farming villages in Taiwan, but does not figure in religious activity in K'un Shen except at *Ch'ing Ming*. When people visit the family graves, they usually *paipai* to the Earth God at the site of the tomb. There is no specific Earth God shrine such as are found in agricultural communities.

---

[1] This god is also a focus of attention for one of the surname groups.

Kuan-kong, who is among other things the god of wealth, can be found in some of the village merchant homes represented by a picture over the altar. Worship is private in these cases. In some households the owners are unable to name the deity whose picture is placed over the altar table. They identify it simply as a Buddha. According to one informant, there is no continuity in keeping one particular god over the family altar. Should the family rebuild their home, or undertake major renovations, it is more than likely that they will select a new picture of a different god to place over the altar. No particular god is deemed appropriate for specific occupations when it comes to the choice of a picture for the households. Embroidered representations of the Eight Immortals are owned by some and decorate the altars or lintels on special occasions such as festivals and weddings. Over the front door some villagers place a round wooden plaque on which is painted a stylized tiger with a sword in his teeth. These are believed to ward off evil spirits and protect the household, but they are not worshipped as gods themselves. They are closer to the concept of spirit soldiers who protect the village.

The villagers also are concerned with deities for whom there are no temples, shrines, cults, or organized celebrations in the village. These are deities who are known by name only, or who may be found in the temples and shrines of neighboring communities. A family may travel to another village to *paipai* such a god in times of crisis, or they may simply invoke the name of the god in order to get help. These usually are gods who are believed to have the power to cure sickness.

The general attitude toward the total pantheon is one of tolerance. "Different villages worship different gods," as one informant put it. There is a bewildering multiplicity of supernatural beings who are approachable by man, but it is not necessary that the individual try to honor each and every one of them, or that the community take cognizance of all the gods. It is enough to select out a few who have universal powers or who have a particular interest in one's own community. Because the gods are not jealous gods, a community will not suffer from divine retribution should it concentrate on a few to the exclusion of the others. The individual becomes concerned with a wider range of gods only in times of crisis, when the gods he is most familiar with fail to solve the problem at hand. Then, he must try other alternatives, and approach gods that he is less familiar with to see if they have the requisite powers to help him. A crisis situation which appears to have been solved by approaching a new god may lead to the incorporation of that god into the village pantheon, as in the examples of *Ong-ia* figures.

The parallel is sometimes drawn between the hierarchy of gods and the hierarchy of government. There are gods with broad powers who are placed at the top of the hierarchy and have authority over other gods and over a wide geographic area. The Jade Emperor falls into this category. Then there are gods like *Co-su-kong* who are equivalent to the district magistrate or a minor local official, whose concern is with the immediate community. There are the wandering gods who approximate the censorate of the former Imperial governmental system, who check on what is happening in the various districts. There are the hosts of spirit soldiers who are the attendant troops to these gods. After this, however, the parallel to government breaks down. The individual and the local community can incorporate still other gods into the system without experiencing a sense of contradiction or strain.

As the villagers see it, there is much work to be done, and sometimes one's "favorite" god cannot do what is requested. The worship of several gods insures that there will be alternatives in a time of need.

Despite the belief in many gods in K'un Shen and the active concern with worshipping them, religion in the community is not conservative in the strict sense of the word. Changes in ritual have occured in the lifetimes of the villagers and changes dictated by economic necessity or "convenience" are acceptable. Gods who were important in the past can fade into oblivion, as some of the worn and forgotten figurines hidden behind the temple altar attest. What remains constant is the belief in the efficacy of a multiplicity of supernatural beings and the broad conception of the proper way to worship and approach them. Most people still wish to preserve the religious tradition. At the same time, they are willing to make changes and revisions within the framework of the system. These, as they work out, may be changes simply in detail, or the admission of a new deity into the system. It is the rare villager who professes a complete lack of faith in the gods and the means of propitiating them, and even the doubters conform under pressure. One woman who assured me that she could not go along with the "superstitions" such as believing in the village gods' power to cure sickness was seen two weeks later at a *tang-ki* seance for her sick child.

The Prevention and Cure of Illness: Sacred and Secular Medicine

The prevention and cure of sickness in K'un Shen combines traditional methods with modern ones. The herbal medicines from the traditional pharmacopoeia are still used, and since the turn of the century, some "Western medicine" and modern sanitation practices have been accepted and integrated into village life. At the same time, divination and appeals to the supernatural for aid still play a large part in the curing or prevention of various ills.

When a person falls ill, the village drugstore is usually the first place he turns to find treatment, assuming that the ailment is a relatively simple one. If a person has the symptoms of a cold, a fever, cough, diarrhea, upset stomach, headache, minor cuts and burns, he depends either on herbal medicines or a variety of patent medicines which are recommended by the druggist or which he already knows from past experiences. An alternative is to purchase a medicine kit from a peddler who comes regularly from the city. The customer's kit is inspected at each visit, and he pays only for the medicines he has used, which are then replaced. Most of the patent medicines in these kits are available from the village drugstore, which also has a much wider range of stock and approximate items found in American drug stores. Most herbal medicines are available only from the druggist and are part of a specialized pharmacopoeia not generally known to the layman. They are purchased from city dealers, and often originate outside of Taiwan. Some herbal medicines can be found growing wild, near the village.

Certain foods are thought to have curative or preventative powers. During the winter months, the eating of snake or goat meat is believed to increase resistance to colds or flu. There are a number of foods which are fever reducers, including lotus root, pineapple juice, and the juice of white turnips. For the fever that accompanies measles, people use coconut milk or winter melon. Cuttlefish soaked in wine is eaten to relieve menstrual pains. Oxtail cooked with garlic is taken for rheumatism. Ginger-root soup is often used for headache. Pork fat or soysauce will be applied to burns, and in the case of dog bite (rare, since there are few dogs in the village) the victim is advised to obtain some rice from the dog's owner, chew it well, and place it on the wound.

Since the end of World War II, a number of Western medicines have become common. Penicillin, in particular, has gained great popularity. Penicillin ointment is easily obtained from the village drugstore, and is used by some families for cuts, scratches, and burns. At the onset of a cold or flu, a number of people now go either to a doctor or to a shot specialist in order to get a penicillin shot. It should be explained that there are people whose main job is to give injections of one or another drug; the village shot specialist in K'un Shen also gives shots to induce abortion. The village school provides smallpox vaccinations and treatment for trachoma. The use of doctors trained in modern medicine has also increased. There is an afternoon clinic, conducted by a doctor who commutes from Tainan for the half-day. It is now felt by many that certain illnesses are best cured by a doctor, if not in the village, then in a city hospital or clinic. These illnesses include tuberculosis, polio, malaria, cholera, meningitis (which is very commonly epidemic among young children), leprosy, flu (Asian and otherwise), diphtheria, serious animal bites, and asthma. Broken bones or sprains are not normally treated by a doctor; there are bone-setters in the city who specialize in this. For a time one of the village barbershops had a dentist.

Of course, there is disagreement as to whether herbal medicines or modern medicines are the more effective. One informant, speaking about treatment of asthma, made the following comment:

> It's not as good to let a Western doctor cure this, because my mother had asthma. Originally she had a Chinese doctor examine her and she took Chinese medicines. But nothing happened at all. Then, she went to a Western doctor who felt that giving her shots would cure her asthma. As a result, when my mother had an asthma attack she was given shots by this Western doctor and died. So it's still safer to have a Chinese doctor treat this illness.

In some illnesses a combination of modern and traditional curing methods are used. Measles, which is quite common in young children, is a case in point. Most families will call in a Western doctor and accept the medicines which he prescribes. At the same time, they give the child a soup of winter melon, often mixed with wild grasses, that have fever-reducing qualities, as part of the medical cure. Juice of white turnips may also be given. Some families buy strengthening herbal compounds from the local drugstore to combat the child's feeling of weakness. The child is kept warmly dressed and wrapped in blankets to help bring the rash out. When the rash has begun to disappear, a ceremony is held in the family's central room. The child is placed on a grass mat or in a bamboo basket in the center of the room. Incense is burned on the altar, and Buddha is asked to "wash away the scars." Until this final ceremony, the child is not allowed out of the house, not for fear that he will infect others, but rather because of the belief that he will become cross-eyed should he chance to see a funeral, wedding, a new mother, or chickens mating. This is the only common childhood disease in which ritual and taboos are reported as a normal part of the curing process. In other diseases, such as whooping cough, the supernatural is invoked only if the disease takes an unusual turn.

If a disease is prolonged, there is recourse to the supernatural. For example, an infant had been ill with digestive troubles for over a week, despite a trip to a doctor and administration of shots. The family then went to visit the temple of *Lin-cui-hu-zin,* who is a special protector of children, and invoked her aid. The evening of the same day, they had their lineage god's small chair brought to their house, and employed sand writing to determine what further aid the child should receive. The interpreter of the chair writing named several wild grasses which the family collected the next day, boiled together in water, and fed to the child. The child's fever went down that day, and a few days later he was completely well, proving to the family that they had indeed wasted time and money by consulting a doctor.

Appeal to the supernatural is also made before illness has a chance to strike. Many children and even some adults wear amulets around the neck consisting of little packets of red cloth in which are contained a piece of paper bearing "magic writing" by the *tang-ki,* or blood collected when he flagellated himself prior to a seance, or ashes from the temple in incense burners. These give general protection. Small children are also presented formally to one or another of the many cult gods as "adopted children," under the god's protection, and there are generalized prayers held at the temple festivals and cult celebrations which ask for protection for all members of the community or congregation.

The occurrence of mental illness is one instance in which solely supernatural means of curing are used. Here, supernatural explanations for the onset are often given, which is not usually the case for the illnesses mentioned previously. It is explained as a result of the breaking of basic moral laws, thus incurring punishment from the gods, or as the result of the actions of a malevolent spirit. In at least one case, it was explained that certain unknown persons invoked an evil god's powers to make a woman insane, and in another case insanity was said to be caused by someone who gave the subject a mirror belonging to an evil spirit; when she looked into it, she went mad. In neither of these two instances have the guilty parties been identified, though attempts have been made to identify the gods and spirits involved in order to make them remove their power. One village insanity case fits into the formula of sorcery. According to village gossip, a woman who married a man from another village was deliberately made insane by her husband, who was not satisfied with her. He took a piece of paper money (ceremonial money), wrote a curse on it, burned it, and mixed the ashes with tea, which he gave her to drink. The result was that she went insane and was then sent home to K'un Shen, where she now lives with her parents. In this case, the person accused of sorcery is an outsider to the village, which may explain the readiness to identify him. No one would ever admit to sorcery occuring with K'un Shen itself. As one informant said,

It's very seldom that a living person will do something to make another person fall ill, because all the people in this village worship good gods. But I've heard that in other villages people worship bad gods, and if someone asks those gods to make trouble for someone, they will. But that can't happen in our village, because our gods are good ones.

There are at least three persons living in the community who are seriously enough disturbed that in American society they would be institutionalized. When they become violent, they are kept locked up at home, even chained, but during their calm periods they are free to participate in daily life as best they can. They often cause laughter, but rarely fear. Their violence is directed mainly at themselves and not at others. One such case is a woman in her late fifties, whose madness is attributed to the "mirror" mentioned earlier. She has lucid periods which last for up to three months at a time. During those times she takes some pains with her appearance and converses reasonably with her neighbors and kin. At other times, however, she becomes intensely depressed, weeps for long periods, refuses to eat, and complains that people are trying to harm her. Sometimes she throws dirty water at people, but has never tried to attack anyone in any other manner. She is cared for by her two married sons, and the general feeling is that she does not need special care such as hospitalization since she is obviously no danger to anyone. She has been ill for 20 years.

Where behavior is aberrant and supernatural causation is suspected, one method of effecting a cure is to invoke the aid of the temple god *Co-su-kong*. The god's carrying chair is brought to the house of the afflicted person, and he or she is made to grasp the poles and follow the chair carriers. The black flag used to call souls and spirits in temple ceremonies is given to the person to wear between their flesh and ordinary clothing. During the curing ceremony, the person, now possessed by the god, is led to a bowl of boiling oil, and his face is pushed into the bowl. According to informants this will not harm the patient because he is protected by the gods, but since I have not seen it done, I cannot validate this. The family and temple personnel then throw handfuls of earth on the person to complete the cure.

Aberrent behavior, particularly in small children, is sometimes explained as temporary soul loss and must be treated in a special way lest it become permanent. For example, one of the village youngsters accidentally fell into a fish pond, from which he was swiftly rescued. However, in the days that followed he cried often, slept poorly, and woke during the night crying. His grandmother realized that through fright he had lost part of his soul, and she led him back to the place where the accident had occurred. With a rice scoop she dipped up water to catch the boy's soul, and then placed the rice basket over his head and called out his given name several times. The paper animal representing the year of the boy's birth was ceremonially burned to represent the transfer of the child's fright to the animal figure. This done, she led him home, the rice basket still over his head so that the spirit would be sure to return home with him. As she explained later, the water had gone out through the holes of the basket, leaving behind only that part of the spirit that was lost.

The belief that a fright does damage to the soul is widespread. If small children and infants are observed to be crying far more than is usual, it is assumed that they have suffered a fright and they can be relieved of it only by ceremonial means. One such ceremony, used after other means to pacify the child have failed, consists of covering a bowl of rice with one of the child's garments and rubbing the covered bowl over the child's hands and feet. Then, the person conducting the ceremony (who can be anyone with expertise—when I observed it, the child's grandmother and one of her friends performed the ceremony) fills his mouth with wine and sprays it over the child's extremities and stomach. Paper money to the gods is burned as the conclusion to the ceremony. Ideally, this should be done immediately after the child has been "frightened," but it is difficult to tell whether it is necessary until a few days have passed.

Emotional disturbances are not the only forms of illness which have a supernatural cause. Any attenuated sickness which fails to respond to various medical techniques will eventually be interpreted as caused by supernatural forces, such as *kui*[2] or various gods. Blindness is very often taken as a sign of punishment for a serious moral breach. Not only may one's own bad behavior lead to such a sickness but also the behavior of one's ancestors may prove to be the cause, for punishments extend down the generations. Events far in the past are believed to be the cause of happenings in the present, and it is here that divination and shamanism must be called into play, to bring to light the underlying cause. Until that cause is made known and measures taken, the patient cannot respond to medication.

Sometimes, it will be found that the causal agent is a person's ancestor who has become angered with his descendants. Failure to conduct proper ancestral memorials turn ancestors into "angry ghosts" who may seek revenge on their descendants. To pacify them, Taoist priests are called in to chant prayers and entreat the gods to hasten the dead soul's entry into a new life, out of the ordeals of hell. The family burns vast quantities of paper money for the dead to facilitate this.

Other times, the cause will prove to be far more complex. For example, there was an elderly woman in the community who had been suffering from heart disease and receiving medical care for it. She consulted one of the village cult gods to seek out the cause, and the *tang-ki* explained that it was because she worried so much. However, the things she worried about had a supernatural cause. The family are fish-pond owners, and recently suffered serious economic losses when the fry in their pond died. The reason for their deaths was revealed to be due to a *kui* of a person buried near the pond. This *kui* was originally from the next fishing village. During his lifetime he was known as a fierce and difficult person who drank heavily and when intoxicated became violent. It was said that he had drowned his ten-year-old son because he felt the child was unfilial. Because of this act, he was abandoned by his relatives and neighbors, and ostracized by the community. He moved to the outskirts of K'un Shen and built a small house for himself. When he died, he was buried at the house site. The house blew down during a typhoon, and eventually it was forgotten. The land was sold and converted into a fish pond. The first owner had a difficult time with the ponds, and was never able to make a profit. The present owners bought the ponds from him, and then suffered serious losses, which presumably brought on the wife's heart trouble. In seance with the *tang-ki* it was revealed that the *kui* felt cheated, and wanted the owner to build a small temple for him. The owner has promised to do so as soon as he has enough money, and has asked the *kui* to give protection to his ponds so that he can raise the money. Pre-

---

[2] *Kui:* A ghost, spirit of the dead, potentially malevolent.

sumably, the wife will recover when this happens, as the source of her worries will have been removed.

Kui can be arbitrary in their choice of victims, unleashing their powers against people who have not personally done them any harm in their lifetime. One such *kui* is the soul of a man who was for a time a Taoist priest. His own wife and sons neglected him in his illness, put him in a wooden shed outside the house, and gave him little food, so that when he died, many people whispered that he had actually starved to death. His burial was a hasty and informal one, and the funeral services abbreviated. As a result, he became a very harmful ghost. His wife and a neighboring woman had quarreled many times, and after his death the neighbor woman became ill, with a disease that no one could diagnose or cure. A seance with the *tang-ki* for *Ong-ia* revealed that her sickness was caused by the dead man's *kui*, and she and her family were urged to make food and incense offerings to his spirit. However, though they did this many times, she did not recover her health. A further seance with *Ong-ia* revealed that even though he and other gods had attempted to restrain the *kui*, they had not been able to do so successfully because he was too powerful. However, no one could explain why the ghost turned on his neighbors instead of his own family.

The only explanation that can be given is that there are those who have a bad fate, a bad fortune already destined for them. The instrument of their undoing does not have to stand in any direct relationship to them and to their own actions. What occurs is, in a sense, foreordained, but not a direct result of something they themselves have done which is now being punished. Causation might perhaps be thought of as a meshwork in which several threads lead to and conjoin at the same interstice and are connected with other threads at other points. There is no simple cause and effect.

The idea of a bad fate is, of course, an explanation that may be invoked in diseases that prove amenable to medical treatment as well as in those cases where the patient fails to respond to treatment from a series of doctors. However, to say "it is fate" and leave it as that is not the proper mode of behavior. One's fate may determine that one falls ill with a particular disease at a particular time, but the individual must still seek a cure, and there is a fair chance that the cure will work. Who can tell, after all, that this is the time that a person is fated to die? As one villager said:

> Man's fate is set. When a person's time comes to die, then no matter what you do, it's no use. But if a person's time to die has not come, then no matter how serious the sickness is, it will not cause him to die. If a person's luck is good, they will get well no matter which doctor treats them. If their luck is not good, then no matter which famous doctor treats them it is useless.

Although there is fatalism in regard to man's destiny and length of life, it admits human efforts as necessary and desirable. Human effort takes two guises. One is the "rational" guise of medicines and preventives against disease. The other is the "religious" guise, the belief that human actions and behavior generally will in some way influence health and life. This latter would include ritual observances toward ancestors and the village gods, morality in daily life, observance of taboos, and the correction of lapses by oneself or one's ancestors through ritual means designed to propitiate the forces that have been upset and angered.

There is disagreement about whether or not the gods directly punish people for moral lapses by causing sickness or death. There is general agreement that evil-doing will eventually be punished, but how and when is another question. For some, the belief is that punishment comes after death in the ordeals of the Buddhist hells. According to others, an individual may escape punishment during his lifetime, but punishment will be visited on his sons or grandsons. Still others believe that retribution will indeed come during the person's lifetime, perhaps shortly after a "visit" to the village by one of the gods who is a wandering censor. After this god has made his report, evildoers will fall ill, unless they sincerely promise that they will never repeat the act and indicate contrition. Occasionally, an act may be so serious in the eyes of the gods that they are not able to escape immediate punishment. To give examples of rapid intervention by the gods:

> About 40 years ago in this village, there was a man and wife. The wife was very jealous because her husband was in love with another man's wife, and she was very unhappy about this. One night, she took some poisoned tea and grain soaked in liquor and put it in the fish pond belonging to that woman's household. The fish all died from the poison. Not long after, she went blind in both eyes. She became blind because what she had done was excessive. She became blind forever.
>
> When [a] woman was in her seventh month there was an opera being shown in her home village, with cloth puppets for the Ghost Festival. Pregnant women are not allowed to watch this kind of opera. But the woman wanted to return home for the day, and watch. Her mother-in-law told her she couldn't, but she was determined to go. And the result was that two days after she came back, the baby died in her womb, because she did not obey her mother-in-law. She was very unhappy, and she didn't dare to tell anyone. By the time that the pain was more than she could bear it was too late for the doctors to do anything, and she died.

The first instance is one of offense against the community. The motif of the person who goes off and secretely poisons someone else's ponds recurs as a stereotypic example of antisocial behavior. It is severely punished in the informant's example, and in later conversation the informant added that the woman was also forced to pay a fine to the family whose pond she had destroyed. In the second example, the offense is the breaking of a religious taboo rather than simple disobedience to a mother-in-law, which seems to be a minor aspect of the offense.

The use of the word "superstition" in reference to religious beliefs now occurs among older members of the community as well as among the younger people being educated in modern schools, particularly with regard to religiomedical practice. The germ theory of disease has some currency, and there are people who posit natural causation for various illnesses. Even so, it does not necessarily undermine the traditional belief system; an explanation in terms of germs and viruses still leaves unanswered the question, "But why me?" People may become convinced of the greater efficacy of new medicines and forsake some of the herbal cures because it seems the more sophisticated and modern thing to do, but the use of divination, shamanistic trance, and propitiation of the gods, ancestors, and ghosts may be long in dying out.

$\boxed{7}$

Conclusions

THE VILLAGE OF K'UN SHEN is but one example drawn from China's myriad "little traditions," but despite certain peculiarities, it is representative. It shares with other Chinese communities such traits as ancestor worship and filial piety, the general subordination of youth and women, allegiance to folk Taoism and Buddhism, and the ideas of moderation in behavior and compromise in interpersonal dealings. Despite the inroads of change, housing, diet, dress, music, and various items of material culture and ideology bear a distinctive Chinese stamp. There are deviations from the ideal model of Chinese culture, particularly in the lesser emphasis placed on kinship, the greater stress placed on individualism, but these deviations are not unique. They relate, in part, to the fact that Taiwan is a lately settled area and in many ways still a frontier. They relate also to the fact that K'un Shen is a fishing village, and has thus been able to remain open to new migrants far longer than agrarian-based communities and to encompass several times the population found in farming villages. Elsewhere in Taiwan there are small and tightly organized villages based on kinship ties and lineage affiliations, but there are also those integrated around patron gods, common locale of origin, and economic cooperation, and comprised of several surname groups. Such communities occurred in mainland China as well.

The proverbial conservatism of the Chinese peasantry appears to be absent from K'un Shen, with little in over-all ideology to block change and modernization. In many ways, the values held by most people in the community are already in line with the demands of an industrializing society. It is with the question of K'un Shen's potential for survival and success in a modernizing nation that these last few pages will be concerned.

As we have seen, the villagers are oriented to time present and future rather than toward the past. No doubt the absence from the village of a gentry/literati class in the past accounts to some extent for this lessened "Confucianization," as does the 50 years of Japanese colonial rule in which new ideas were slowly introduced and assimilated. So too does the recognition of what the past represents in

108

terms of poverty and low social status. In the economic sphere, strict adherance to traditionalism in and of itself is rejected. It is perceived as dysfunctional.

The Confucian teachings which restrict women's place to within the household have also received little support in the past, both because of economic necessity and because of the work ethic. Women now, as in the past, work outside of the household, bring in a cash income, and play a role, albeit a subordinate one, in family and community actions. Although their participation is not equal to that of men, they have considerably more freedom and responsibility than the Confucian model for behavior would recommend. The way has been eased for them to take jobs in the new city shops and factories.

Long and hard hours of work are not perceived as something to be avoided. The distaste and disdain for manual labor and the desire for leisure which characterized the gentry and rich peasantry of the Mainland do not seem to have taken root in this village. And the work ethic is closely related to the individualism evident among the villagers. Life is a constant and often difficult struggle to maintain a small household. Rarely is cooperation extended automatically among kinsmen. The values of the community hold that a man's first responsibilities are to his wife and children and to aged parents without means of support, but his grown brothers should be able to fend for themselves, and feelings of responsibility are even weaker toward more remote collateral kin. Values such as these make mobility possible, and as new industries develop in the urban centers,. we would expect a relatively painless change in occupation. The nearness to the city and ease of commuting may make less necessary a change of residence, but should commuting prove tedious, the nuclear-family households can detach themselves from the village with less psychic cost than that paid by the members of the rarer extended-family households.

The transition to the modern world is also eased by the villager's view of the natural world and man's place within it, particularly the view that man does have some control over nature and can better his life through improved knowledge and skills. The religious beliefs current in the community do not present a serious barrier to acceptance of change. In the area of health, the system has proved flexible enough to allow the incorporation of new methods of curing and preventing of disease. More generally, scientific knowledge introduced from the Western world is seen as an increment to knowledge rather than a blanket refutation of traditional beliefs. Man does his share; the gods do their share. Success in various ventures is dependent on both, with perhaps a heavier weighting of human effort over supernatural interventions. The new word, "science," has taken on very positive connotations, and fatalistic attitudes are dying out.

Although dramatic changes have not yet occurred within the village, there is an eagerness for certain kinds of change such as improvements in the standard of living, the taking on of new occupations (particularly among the young people), and the learning of ideas that will make the village "modern" or "progressive" when viewed by the rest of Taiwanese society. The word "change," like "science," has also acquired a positive connotation. Only to some of the older people is it a negatively charged word as they lament that the festivals are less lively than they remember them from their youth, that the children and young people are less polite, that the girls have too much freedom, that somehow good things are being lost along with the bad. However, these are usually brushed aside as the complaints of overly conservative oldsters.

Life has not yet been disrupted by the process of modernization. Population has continued to increase over the past few decades and despite some permanent emigration, life in the village is still thought preferable to urban slum dwelling. Compromises have alleviated some of the tensions between generations, particularly in the area of marriage arrangements. Primary education is gradually being accepted as a necessity for both sexes, and as the government makes middle-school education accessible to a larger percentage of youth (as it is now doing), support and enthusiasm for the village school will probably increase. Although the fishing industry is dying due to ecological factors and lack of mechanization, new uses are being found for community resources. In the last few years, some of the villagers have become involved in developing the beach as a recreation area for "tourists." Gradually, the village is entering the modern world, while retaining much of its traditional life style.

Recommended Reading

FAIRBANK, JOHN KING, 1958, *The United States and China*. Cambridge, Mass.: Harvard University Press.

A concise and authoritative discussion of traditional institutions, historical background, and twentieth century developments in China by an outstanding historian.

FEI, HSIAO TUNG, 1939, *Peasant Life in China*. London: Routledge & Kegan Paul, Ltd.

A classic study of a village in eastern China under the pressures and problems of a changing economy. Includes some material on fishermen.

FREEDMAN, MAURICE, 1958, *Lineage Organization in Southeastern China*. London: The Athlone Press.

A descriptive analysis of household, family, and lineage in traditional China, particularly the Fukien–Kwangtung area.

FRIED, MORTON H., 1953, *The Fabric of Chinese Society*. New York: Praeger, Inc.

An excellent account of family and nonkin ties that hold together the landlords, peasants, merchants, and artisans in and around a marketing town in central China.

GALLIN, BERNARD, 1966, *Hsin Hsing, Taiwan: A Chinese Village in Change*. Berkeley and Los Angeles: University of California Press.

An ethnographic study of a Hokkien farming village in central Taiwan. Includes material on the effects of the land-reform program and recent economic growth.

KERR, GEORGE H., 1965, *Formosa Betrayed*. Boston: Houghton Mifflin Company.

A former Embassy official's observations on political events in Taiwan since its return to Nationalist China.

MYRDAL, JAN, 1965, *Report from a Chinese Village*. New York: Pantheon Books, Inc.

A valuable description of life in a Shensi village in the 1960s, by a journalist/sociologist. Contains a wealth of firsthand accounts of peasant life before and after the Communist revolution.

POTTER, JACK M., 1968, *Capitalism and the Chinese Peasant*. Berkeley and Los Angeles: University of California Press.

An ethnography which focuses on the social and cultural effects of economic change in a farming village in the New Territories (Hong Kong). Critical of the hypotheses of Fei and other Chinese social scientists.

WOLF, MARGERY, 1968, *The House of Lim*. New York: Appleton-Century-Crofts.

A sensitive and beautifully written study of a Taiwanese farm family over several generations, using a life-history approach.

YANG, MARTIN, 1945, *A Chinese Village: Taitou, Shantung Province*. New York: Columbia University Press.

A comprehensive ethnographic study of the author's home village, containing data on family life, village organization, economics, and religion in a relatively conservative peasant community.